Assassination in Colonial Cyprus in 1934 and the Origins of EOKA

Assassination in Colonial Cyprus in 1934 and the Origins of EOKA

Reading the Archives against the Grain

Andrekos Varnava

ANTHEM PRESS

Anthem Press
An imprint of Wimbledon Publishing Company
www.anthempress.com

This edition first published in UK and USA 2021
by ANTHEM PRESS
75–76 Blackfriars Road, London SE1 8HA, UK
or PO Box 9779, London SW19 7ZG, UK
and
244 Madison Ave #116, New York, NY 10016, USA

Copyright © Andrekos Varnava 2021

The author asserts the moral right to be identified as the author of this work.

All rights reserved. Without limiting the rights under copyright reserved above,
no part of this publication may be reproduced, stored or introduced into
a retrieval system, or transmitted, in any form or by any means
(electronic, mechanical, photocopying, recording or otherwise),
without the prior written permission of both the copyright
owner and the above publisher of this book.

British Library Cataloguing-in-Publication Data
A catalogue record for this book is available from the British Library.

Library of Congress Control Number: 2020952090

ISBN-13: 978-1-78527-552-4 (Pbk)
ISBN-10: 1-78527-552-6 (Pbk)

Cover image: Photo of Antonios Triantafyllides,
Vassiliou Studio, Limassol, 1928. Courtesy of the Monica (Mona) Soteriades
Archive at Library of the Cyprus University of Technology, Limassol, Cyprus.

This title is also available as an e-book.

To Antonios Triantafyllides, b. 1890, d. 1934: With this book I hope now you can rest in peace. May your memory be eternal, and your voice and legacy an exemplar to others.

To the Triantafyllides family: I hope that this detailed account and analysis can bring you some further closure and comfort in the knowledge that Antonios Triantafyllides was ahead of his time and on the right side of history.

Photo of the Grave of Antonios Triantafyllides, 2020.

Source: © Dr Nicholas Coureas, Cyprus Research Centre, Nicosia, Cyprus.

CONTENTS

List of Figures ix
Acknowledgements xi
List of Abbreviations xv
Note on Translations xvii

Introduction 1

1. Triantafyllides before his Assassination 23
2. The Colonial Newspaper Archive and the Triantafyllides Case 47
3. The Colonial Government Archive and the Triantafyllides Case 61
4. The Assassination of Triantafyllides and the EOKA Connection 85

Conclusion 103

Select Bibliography 111
Index 121

FIGURES

1.1 Photo of Antonios Triantafyllides in 1919, J.P. Foscolo Studio. *Source:* Courtesy of Dr Nicholas Coureas, Nicosia, Cyprus. 26
1.2 Triantafyllides with other members of the Legal Fraternity, 1927. *Source:* Courtesy of Agni Michaelidou, Χώρα, η Παληά Λευκωσία (Country, Old Nicosia), Nicosia, 1974. 29
1.3 (above) 'Ο ΛΑΙΚΟΣ ΚΑΤΑΔΙΩΚΟΜΕΝΟΣ ΥΠΟ ΤΟΥ ΛΑΟΥ ΤΟΥ (below) Αχ! αυτά τα αγκάθια τις τριανταφυλλιάς με κατέστρεψαν ((above) THE POPULIST CHASED BY THEIR PEOPLE (below) Ah! these rose thorns have ruined me). Cartoon from the 1930 elections for the Legislative Council, depicting Hadji Pavlou being chased into thorny rose bushes by peasants and labourers supporting Triantafyllides, Κύπρος (Cyprus), Limassol, 1930. *Source:* Courtesy of Stelios A. Triantafyllides, Nicosia, Cyprus. 31
1.4 Sir Reginald Edward Stubbs, c. 1925. *Source:* Government Public Record Office, Hong Kong. Photo in the public domain according to Section 17 in Chapter 528 (Copyright Ordinance) of the Law of Hong Kong. 41
2.1 Antonios Triantafyllides, Vassiliou Studio, Limassol, 1928. Photo appeared in *Φωνή της Κύπρου*, 20 January 1934. *Source:* Courtesy of Stelios A. Triantafyllides, Nicosia, Cyprus. 50
3.1 Sir Herbert Richmond Palmer, 1924. *Source:* Family Archives licensed under the Creative Commons Attribution-Share Alike 3.0. 62

ACKNOWLEDGEMENTS

This is my fourth monograph and the most difficult to research and write, although shorter than the other three. Difficult because of the sense of responsibility to present who was seemingly behind the assassination of Antonios Triantafyllides. There can be no denying the controversial subject, but there cannot be any fear of attempting to find the truth, even if, as historians, there is always uncertainty over the truth.

Without archives, a historical record cannot be reconstructed. I start by thanking the archives and libraries that I have utilised: the National Archives of the UK, London; the Bodleian Library, Special Collections, University of Oxford; the State Archives, Nicosia; and the National Library of Australia. I also thank the newspaper archives held at the Public Information Office in Nicosia and my initial research assistant Marios Siammas and lately Nikos Christofi. I also thank Rita Severis from the *Costas and Rita Severis Foundation* for kindly providing me with the relevant pages from the diary of Sir Henry Blackall. I also thank the Flinders University Library document delivery staff for obtaining some obscure sources. Finally, thank you to Stelios A. Triantafyllides for making available his personal archive on his grandfather.

This research has had incredible support and feedback, arguably more than my previous monographs. As this project began as a journal article, it received four anonymous reports, and before submissions I sent various versions to numerous scholars. This was largely because of the controversial nature of the research and my apprehension at my findings. I warmly thank the following, listed in no particular order: Kim Economides (and for invaluable legal advice), Tim Reardon, Alexis Rappas, Yiannos Katsourides, Evan Smith, Matthew Fitzpatrick, John Burke, Nicholas Doumanis, Panikos Panayi, Andonis Piperoglou, Marios Siammas, Antonis Hadjikyriakou, Michael J. K. Walsh, Hubert Faustmann (and for the Richter reference), Romain Fathi, Alexios Alecou, Marina Marangos and Nicholas Coureas. Apologies to anyone who I have forgotten. I single out Nicholas Coureas for his unrelenting encouragement and willingness to speak about whatever information he was given by his family, as well as the effort he made in the last months to copy material, photograph the grave of Antonios Triantafyllides and make phone calls for me in Cyprus. Thank you also to the numerous people with whom I discussed this research and case, and for their willingness to help, share rumours and offer encouragement and support.

I must also thank the conferences and seminar organisers that accepted or invited me to deliver my research on the assassination of Antonios Triantafyllides. In November 2016, I first presented my research on the case at the 'Colonial Formations: Connections and Collisions' conference held at the University of Wollongong, NSW, and I was thrilled by the interest and useful questions and comments. I must thank the then School of History and International Relations at Flinders University for funding that trip. I next presented this research to the history research community at Flinders University on 24 March 2017, and received the wonderful feedback and thought-provoking questions. So, thank you to the group on that particular day and on other days, given the many conversations over lunch, coffee and in the corridors. And finally, I was honoured to have been invited by Saliha Belmessous to present this research at the history seminar series at the University of New South Wales on 4 September 2018 and was thrilled by the thought-provoking comments and questions.

I must also thank the four anonymous reviewers who reported on the earlier article versions for the two journals. Three of these reviews were exceedingly positive. The only negative reviewer called me an 'anti-nationalist' and was critical of my mentioning fascism in Cyprus in the 1930s. Needless to say that such an ideological contamination of the peer review process is unfortunate and only served to spur me on further, although it was a blow at the time.

Thanks also to Anthem Press, who had the courage to pursue this project. I am thankful to Marie Ruiz, the editor of the series, for her encouragement. To my editor, Megan Greiving, thank you for handling the process so professionally and for being flexible with last minute changes. And, finally, to the six anonymous reviewers (across two rounds of review) and the academic adviser for their positive suggestions, which led to far more digging and a considerably improved manuscript.

Finally, but not least, I thank my family for their understanding, support and patience. Being a scholar can be all-consuming and a subject like this can be even more so. It involves significant travel, in this case both international and interstate, and being away from family. Much has transpired over the years of working on what began as a little project. In 2019, I lost my dad. I want to thank both my parents for their support in allowing me to pursue the career of my dreams. To my wife Helen, thanks for your patience and support with me being away on multiple research and conference trips, for contributing to many conversations about this mysterious assassination, and sorry for the times I tuned out when you were trying to talk to me about something and my mind wandered off to think about some aspect of this case. I also want to thank Antonis Pitrakkou, my wife's uncle, for the many long talks about his memories of the assassination of Antonios Triantafyllides. And also a big thank you to everyone else in my family for your support.

Needless to say, any errors are my own. Indeed, the theory presented here may be wrong, but all historical reconstruction can be. Growing up I loved watching 'Columbo' and 'Matlock' crime dramas, but this is not my effort to live out any TV crime drama. I am thoroughly aware of the seriousness of the claims in this book, but after 87 years the time has come to shed some light on this assassination, which has had and continues to have serious consequences for Cyprus. I am comfortable that I have consulted all the evidence and sources available and I am comfortable in my analysis, no matter how controversial some people may believe it to be.

Kantara House, Adelaide,
22 June 2020

ABBREVIATIONS

The entries are mainly to assist in deciphering acronyms in the footnotes. Sometimes for 'Assistant' or 'Acting' an 'A' has been added, for example Acting Chief Secretary (ACS) and these are not listed below.

AKEL	*Ανορθωτικό Κόμμα Εργαζόμενου Λαού* (Progressive Party of Working People)
APOEL	*Αθλητικός Ποδοσφαιρικός Όμιλος Ελλήνων Λευκωσίας* (Athletic Football Club of the Greeks of Nicosia)
CCPC	Chief Commandant of Police, Cyprus (Cypriot Military Police – *Zaptieh*)
CGPO	Cyprus Government Printing Office
CIA	Central Intelligence Agency
CMP	Cypriot Military Police (*Zaptieh*)
CO	Colonial Office
CPC	*Κομμουνιστικό Κόμμα Κύπρου* (Communist Party of Cyprus) – English acronym so as to not confuse Greek acronym of KKK with Ku Klux Klan
CSC	Chief Secretary/Colonial Secretary (from 1926) – Cyprus
DCFam	District Commissioner of Famagusta
DCNic	District Commissioner of Nicosia
EOKA	*Εθνική Οργάνωσης Κυπρίων Αγωνιστών* (National Organisation of Cypriot Fighters)
EREK	*Εθνική Ριζοσπαστική Ένωσις Κύπρου* (National Radical Union of Cyprus)
ERE	*Εθνική Ριζοσπαστική Ένωσις* (National Radical Union) – Greece
FBIS	Foreign Broadcast Information Service
FCO	Foreign and Commonwealth Office
FIFA	*Fédération Internationale de Football Association* (International Federation of Association Football)
FO	Foreign Office
GoC	Government of Cyprus/Governor of Cyprus
HoC	House of Commons

HCC	High Commissioner of Cyprus
KEK	*Κυπριακόν Εθνικόν Κόμμα* (Cypriot Nationalist Party)
LCCCID	Local Commandant of Cypriot Crime Investigation Department
NAUK	National Archives of the United Kingdom (Kew Gardens, London)
NLC	National Liberation Coalition
OCTE	Officer Commanding the Troops in Egypt
RDP	Remote Desktop Protocol
SA1	Secretariat Archives (State Archives, Nicosia)
TMT	*Türk Mukavemet Teşkilatı* (Turkish Resistance Organisation)
SSC	Secretary of State for the Colonies
WO	War Office

NOTE ON TRANSLATIONS

All translations from Greek to English are either by the Cypriot government, which I have checked with the original (and have always found the translations, which were the work of extremely experienced local Cypriots, to be of the highest quality), or they are my own translations.

INTRODUCTION

And the truth shall set you free.
Bible, John, Chapter 8, verse 32.

After a long and hard day's work, partly in Larnaca, Antonios Triantafyllides, a leading Cypriot lawyer recently appointed to the government's new advisory council, arrived at his Nicosia home in the cool evening of 12 January 1934, only to be met with an assassin's bullets. He died the next morning. Twelve months later, Stavros Christodoulou was charged, but acquitted of murder. The assassination is a taboo subject for Cypriot society and historians alike, and a cold case that nobody has seemingly wanted to explore, until now.

This is true even when on 1 February 2002 Antonios's son, Michalakis A. Triantafyllides, made startling revelations in an interview on who was behind the assassination. Michalakis acknowledged that much was rumoured about it, but after discovering the 'British file' left in Cyprus, he found that his father had been a trusted friend of the Greek prime minister, Eleftherios Venizelos, and had decided to follow, along with others, the advice of Venizelos to cooperate with the British to achieve their acceptance of the union of Cyprus with Greece (*enosis*). This angered a group of 'raging fanatics' from Kyrenia, who claimed that such cooperation would kill *enosis*. To prevent this, they decided to assassinate one of the men cooperating with the British. They put four names in a hat, Antonios's 'trusted' physician drew his name out and they paid someone to do it. Michalakis was careful not to mention any names, but left little to the imagination, by referring to the 'raging fanatics' from Kyrenia and that the man accused of the shooting in court later approached him for forgiveness. When he was Attorney General (i.e., 1988–95) he was informed that the assassin was dying of cancer and that he wanted Michalakis to forgive him. Michalakis does not say if he visited him, but he did forgive him in a public statement, which the assassin did not appreciate and issued legal proceedings, forcing Michalakis to publish an apology. Clearly, he did not want the publicity of a libel case.[1]

Despite what Michalakis stated in that interview there are still many unanswered questions, inconsistencies and gaps, and the subject remains controversial. In 2011 the Foreign and Commonwealth Office (FCO) circulated a list of files (from the policy code-named 'Operation Legacy', or the so-called migrated files), including: 'Cyprus: Assassination of Antonios Triantafyllides, Nicosia member of the Advisory Council', which triggered my investigation. There was no file at the Cypriot State Archives on the assassination (the file listed as being there was this FCO file), so Michalakis Triantafyllides may have been referring to another file with the dossiers of the men interned in connection with the assassination.[2] The FCO file was to remain closed until 2034. My first request to open it was rejected in 2012, but an appeal succeeded, though six pages were extracted and others were redacted. I then submitted an article, which was rejected about 12 months later. After a hiatus, I tried to have the entire file opened. Between June 2018 and July 2019, this was the subject of a Freedom of Information request, when they were finally released. Then I submitted the revised article to another journal and it was also rejected. Clearly, the story remains controversial and not merely for Cypriots.

This book offers a theory on who was behind the assassination of Antonios Triantafyllides, testing the information provided by Michalakis. In so doing it explores the relationship between the British colonial authorities and the Cypriot political elites, and the various divisions within the latter on how to pursue 'national liberation'. To achieve this, it first creates a 'community of records' from official colonial files and local colonial and regional newspapers, and analyses these both with and against the grain. Triantafyllides supported *enosis*, but after almost two decades of involvement in pro-*enosis* nationalist politics without results (in fact, the opposite) he decided that the only way to achieve it was to not antagonise the British, but to work with them. This change occurred owing to the 1931 crisis, which culminated in the burning of Government House in Nicosia in October and led to a British crackdown, including the suspension of the constitution, abolition of the legislative council, the imposition of press censorship and the deporting of leading nationalists and communists implicated directly or indirectly in the events. After this, Triantafyllides and others were more acceptable of the view of the Greek prime minister, Eleftherios Venizelos, that to achieve *enosis* the Greek

---

[1] Michalakis Triantafyllides interview, 1 February 2002, in Antigoni Solomonidou-Drousiotou, *Η Ζωή μου σε Πρώτο Πρόσωπο* [My Life in the First Person] (Athens, Livani, 2004), 33–41.

[2] State Archives, Nicosia, Secretariat Archive 1 (SA1), SA1/438/34.

Cypriots needed to convince the British of its feasibility and desirability. In October 1933 the British established an advisory council of leading Cypriots. Triantafyllides, who had, albeit briefly, served in the elected legislative council and the nominated executive council, became a member. He attended the first meeting before being shot. The British initially suspected the pro-*enosis* extremists and interned five, then at the court proceedings blamed a communist conspiracy, but the man charged was acquitted. This is now an 87-year-old cold case and this is the first attempt to offer an explanation.

After creating and analysing a 'community of records', this book shows that by reading both with and especially against the grain it is probable that those responsible were far right pro-*enosis* extremists. Thus, for historical criminologists and crime investigators, the exploration of the sources could be a model for forensic analysis of cold cases. For those interested in the British Empire, the book shows how the British authorities had no control over extremist nationalist politics and political violence in the 1930s, any more than they did in the 1950s, and they were unable to protect those willing to work with them to better the country. In fact, as numerous historians have attested, during the EOKA (*Εθνική Οργάνωσις Κυπρίων Αγωνιστών* – National Organisation of Cypriot Fighters) campaign between April 1955 and March 1959, more Greek Cypriot civilians were murdered than any other target group.[3] For Cypriots and others interested in Cypriot history, this book will make startling and uncomfortable revelations about the so-called national liberation movement. It will suggest that the violence that gripped the island from the 1950s and led to partition could have been avoided had it not been for the assassination of one of the most intelligent, popular and incisive politicians produced in Cyprus until that time and those seemingly responsible not getting away with it to do it again. This last point is because they did get away with it, since the book establishes a line of descent between some of those men seemingly behind the assassination who later created EOKA, showing that violence was inherent in their politics, and how the failure to punish them led to the unhealthy role of the far right in Cyprus.

Historiography

The assassination of Triantafyllides has been silenced from the history of the colonial and anti-colonial projects in Cyprus. An inclusive Cypriot

---

[3] Nancy Crawshaw, *The Cyprus Revolt* (London: George Allen & Unwin, 1978), 175, 190, 244–55, 257, 280–82, 315–17, 406; David French, *Fighting EOKA: The British Counter-Insurgency Campaign on Cyprus, 1955–1959* (Oxford: Oxford University Press, 2015), 89–90, 110–11, 159–70, 281, 294–95.

historiography appeared in the 1990s.⁴ Before then the histories of Cyprus merely focused on the nationalisms of the two main communities, giving nationalist interpretations to historical events. Even the few exceptions were political, for instance the 'peaceful co-existence thesis' of Costas Kyrris, which claimed that the Greek and Turkish Cypriots had always 'peacefully coexisted' to counter the geographical separation policy of the Turkish Cypriot leadership and Turkey, which succeeded in 1974.⁵ The development of political modernity in Cyprus was stunted after the events in October 1931, as representative institutions were never reintroduced, despite British efforts after the Second World War.⁶ The advisory council introduced in 1933 was the first step towards a new constitution, but was set back with Triantafyllides's assassination. Triantafyllides represented another path towards *enosis* or liberation, the longer constitutional path, working with the British, such as the Maltese

---

⁴ Rolandos Katsiaounis, *Labour, Society and Politics in Cyprus during the Second Half of the Nineteenth Century* (Nicosia: Cyprus Research Centre, 1996); Rebecca Bryant, *Imagining the Modern: The Cultures of Nationalism in Cyprus* (London: I.B. Tauris, 2004); Andrekos Varnava, *British Imperialism in Cyprus, 1878–1915: The Inconsequential Possession* (Manchester: Manchester University Press, 2009); Andrekos Varnava, *Serving the Empire in the Great War: The Cypriot Mule Corps, Imperial Loyalty and Silenced Memory* (Manchester: Manchester University Press, 2017); Andrekos Varnava, *British Cyprus and the Long Great War, 1914–1925: Empire, Loyalties and Democratic Deficit* (London: Routledge, 2020).

⁵ Costas Kyrris, 'Symbiotic Elements in the History of the Two Communities of Cyprus', *Kypriakos Logos* 8 (1976): 243–82; Costas Kyrris, *Peaceful Co-existence in Cyprus under British Rule (1878–1959) and after Independence* (Nicosia: PIO, 1977). Costas Kyrris was a rightwing nationalist trade unionist in his 20s, see NAUK, FCO141/4281, top secret, KEK Dossier, 1949. Yiannis Papadakis, 'The Politics of Memory and of Forgetting in Cyprus', *Journal of Mediterranean Studies* 3, no. 1 (1993): 139–54; Yiannis Papadakis, 'Greek Cypriot Narratives of History and Collective Identity: Nationalism as a Contested Process', *American Ethnologist* 25, no. 3 (1998): 149–65; Stavroula Philippou and Andrekos Varnava, 'Constructions of Solution(s) to the Cyprus Problem: Exploring Formal Curricula in Greek-Cypriot State Schools', in *Reunifying Cyprus: The Annan Plan and Beyond*, ed. Andrekos Varnava and Hubert Faustmann (London: I.B. Tauris, 2009), 194–212; Andrekos Varnava and Michalis N. Michael, 'Archbishop-Ethnarchs since 1767', in *The Archbishops of Cyprus in the Modern Age: The Changing Role of the Archbishop-Ethnarch, Their Identities and Politics*, ed. Andrekos Varnava and Michalis Michael (Newcastle upon Tyne: Cambridge Scholars Publishing, 2013), 1–16.

⁶ Andrekos Varnava and Christalla Yakinthou, 'Cyprus: Political Modernity and Structures of Democracy in a Divided Island', in *The Oxford Handbook of Local and Regional Democracy in Europe*, ed. John Loughlin, Frank Hendriks, and Anders Lidström (Oxford: Oxford University Press, 2011), 455–77. For British efforts at reintroducing constitutional government see Rolandos Katsiaounis, *Η Διασκεπτική, 1946–1948: Με Ανασκόπηση της Περιόδου, 1878–1945* [The Consultative Assembly, 1946–48: With a Survey of the Period, 1878–1945] (Nicosia: Cyprus Research Centre, 2000); Yiorghos Leventis, *Cyprus: The Struggle for Self-Determination in the 1940s* (Frankfurt: Peter Lang, 2002).

did, which may have been more successful than EOKA's violent one. It is not shocking that the book draws a line of descent between those who seemingly plotted Triantafyllides's assassination and their role in founding EOKA, or that two other murders also may be linked to them.

These connections help explain why this is a silenced and distorted event within Cypriot national consciousness and virtually from historical accounts. Hill revealed that the men who had agreed to serve on the advisory council were branded as traitors and that one, Antonios Triantafyllides, was assassinated. The suspected motive was political, 'although no impeachable evidence to that effect was forthcoming'.[7] He added in a footnote that Triantafyllides's father-in-law, Theophanis Theodotou, had evidence that Triantafyllides had been 'threatened with assassination if he continued to serve on the advisory council'.[8] Purcell claimed that Triantafyllides was 'assassinated', without elaborating further.[9] Georghallides's books and articles offer context on Triantafyllides's role in public life and on the radical nationalists hostile to him, but neither book explores the assassination because he stopped with the end of the governorship of Sir Ronald Storrs in 1932.[10] In Greek, the 1980 book by Ioannis Pikros on Venizelos and the Cyprus 'problem' provides useful background, but his analysis gives little insight into the role or assassination of Triantafyllides.[11] Recent books on the 1930s and the rise of left-wing and right-wing politics

---

[7] Sir George Francis Hill, *A History of Cyprus*, IV (ed.) Sir Harry Luke (Cambridge University Press, 1952), 432–33. Hill was one of only two historians to note that the press censorship had been relaxed in 1933 and only reimposed after the assassination of Triantafyllides. Ibid., 553. The other was Petros Stylianou, *Το Κίνημα του Οκτώβρη του 1931 στην Κύπρο* [The Movement of October of 1931 in Cyprus] (Nicosia: P. Stylianou, 1984), 232.

[8] Hill, *A History of Cyprus*, 433. Hill's knowledge of Theodotou's evidence indicates that he (or Luke) had spoken with Theodotou and/or with others who knew of his views or had seen Theodotou's letters.

[9] H. D. Purcell, *Cyprus* (London: Ernest Benn, 1969), 225.

[10] George Georghallides, *A Political and Administrative History of Cyprus* (Nicosia: Cyprus Research Centre, 1979); George Georghallides, *Cyprus and the Governorship of Sir Ronald Storrs: The Causes of the 1931 Crisis* (Nicosia: Cyprus Research Centre, 1985); George Georghallides, 'The Cyprus Revolt and the British Deportation Policy, October 1931-December 1932', *Kypriakai Spoudai* (1993): 37–114; George Georghallides, 'Church and State in Cyprus, October 1931 to November 1932: A Systematic Humiliation of the Autocephalous Church of Cyprus?' *Annual of the Cyprus Research Centre* 19 (1992): 361–448; George Georghallides, 'British Policy on Cyprus During 1931', *Πρακτικά του Πρώτου Διεθνούς Κυπριολογικού Συνεδρίου, Λευκωσία 14–19 Απριλίου 1969* [First International Conference of Cypriot Studies, Nicosia 14–19 April 1969], 3(A) (Nicosia, 1973), 96–104.

[11] Yiannis Pikros, *Ο Βενιζέλος και το Κυπριακό* [Venizelos and the Cyprus 'Problem'] (Athens, Filippoti), 1980.

do not mention the assassination.¹² Three others refer to the assassination as a 'murder', thus giving credence to the 'personal motive' narrative created at the time by the far right extremists who were probably behind it.¹³ Finally, the 2019 book by Christos P. Ioannides, the son of Polycarpos Ioannides, one of the men at the centre of this account. Unsurprisingly he failed to mention who his father was, his involvement in far right politics, or the assassination of Triantafyllides. Further, he erroneously claimed that the secret nationalist society, which became EREK *"Εθνική Ριζοσπαστική Ένωσις Κυπρου"* (National Radical Union of Cyprus) in October 1931, which consisted of the men at the centre of this case, was non-violent and took inspiration from Mahatma Gandhi, who would be rolling in his grave at this.¹⁴

The only sustained commentary on the assassination of Triantafyllides was from Panayiotis Papademetris 40 years ago. Papademetris was a journalist, first with *Μάχη* (Battle) in the 1960s, the newspaper of the EOKA gunman, paramilitary leader and subsequent president of the coup in 1974, Nicos Sampson, and ending with *Αγών* (Struggle) in 1998, the newspaper of another EOKA cadre and paramilitary figure, Nicos Koshis, who was the Minister of Justice from 1997. His six pages were mostly from *Ελευθερία* (Freedom), since he liberally quotes from its reports of the trial and included four of its sketches. Papademetris accepted that Triantafyllides was assassinated, but the motives were not determined and the assassin was not found. He showed that the accused, Stavros Christodoulou, had admitted to lying and giving false statements to obtain the £1,000 reward so he could pay the lawyer who had previously represented him in his case of attempted murder.¹⁵ Although, in the late 1970s, Papademetris did not have access to all the documents and was a right-wing nationalist, he must be credited for saying anything at all.

---

[12] Leventis, *Cyprus*; Alexis Rappas, *Cyprus in the 1930s: British Colonial Rule and the Roots of the Cyprus Conflict* (London: I.B. Tauris, 2014); Yiannos Katsourides, *The History of the Communist Party in Cyprus* (London: I.B. Tauris, 2014); Yiannos Katsourides, *The Greek Cypriot Nationalist Right in the Era of British Colonialism* (Cham, Switzerland: Springer, 2017).

[13] Heinz Richter, *Geschichte der Insel Zypern, 1878–1949* (History of the Island of Cyprus, 1878–1949), Vol. 1 (Mannheim and Möhnesee: Bibliopolis, 2004), 336; Antigone Heraclidou, *Imperial Control in Cyprus: Education and Political Manipulation in the British Empire* (International Library of Twentieth Century History) (London: I.B. Tauris, 2017), 58; Diana Markides, *The Cyprus Tribute and Geopolitics in the Levant, 1875–1960* (Cham, Switzerland: Palgrave Macmillan, 2019), 159, 179.

[14] Christos P. Ioannides, *Cyprus under British Colonial Rule* (Lanham: Lexington, 2019), 173–74.

[15] Panayiotis Papademetris, *Ιστορική Εγκυκλοπαίδεια της Κύπρου, 1878–1978* [Historical Encyclopaedia of Cyprus, 1878–1978], Vol. 2, on 1931–1946 (Nicosia, 1979–80), 170–75. Also http://www.papademetris.net/index.php?option=com_content&view=article&id=1125:s-569&catid=114:1931-1938-4&Itemid=114

Finally, two useful dissertations covering different aspects of the period and discussing, albeit briefly, the assassination. Thomas Papageorgiou provided invaluable information on the activities of the deported Cypriot figures in Athens who are at the heart of this book. On the assassination of Triantafyllides, he consulted CO67/253/10 and CO67/253/11, but not the relevant FCO files or others connected to the case. He thus could not provide a comprehensive picture, yet he did report faithfully the view from Theodotou that the assassination was organised by the deported figures in Athens, Savvas Loizides, Bishop Makarios of Kyrenia and others.[16] Athanasios Voudouris's dissertation provided further insights into the 'Church Question' between 1933 and 1947, particularly as regards the fanatical supporters of Makarios, while it claimed that Triantafyllides was assassinated for political reasons in response to British autocratic measures and because he was considered 'a traitor' for cooperating with them. Nothing was mentioned about the British view that one of the motives for his assassination was Triantafyllides's views on the 'Church Question', since they were not presented.[17]

Theoretical Framework

This study criss-crosses several theoretical contexts. It is a story of the British Mediterranean experience of Empire, that is, Gibraltar, Malta, Cyprus, Egypt, and Palestine. It is a developing field over the last two decades, which needs to contrast and compare across places more. It is specifically about the imperial encounter, moving forward the scholarship from Robinson's seminal piece forty-odd years ago.[18] Triantafyllides embodied both resistance to and cooperation with the colonial authorities. As a supporter of *enosis*, he opposed British rule, while as an advisor he cooperated. He did not see his embodiment of resistance and cooperation as opposites, since he believed that *enosis* or liberation could only be achieved by cooperating with the British to develop the island and convince the British of its feasibility. But this is not how his enemies

---

[16] Thomas Papageorgiou, *Η Κυπριακή Ενωτική Κίνηση στην Αθήνα, 1931–1940: Οι Βρετανικές Αντιδράσεις και η Στάση των Ελληνικών Κυβερνήσεων* [The Cyprus *Enosis* Movement in Athens, 1931–1940: The British Reaction and the Attitude of the Greek Governments], unpublished PhD dissertation (Aristotle University of Thessaloniki, 2014), 114, 228–29, 286–87.

[17] Athanasios G. Voudouris, *Το Εκκλησιαστικό Ζήτημα της Κύπρου κατά την Περίοδο 1933–1947* [The Church Question of Cyprus during the Period 1933–1947], unpublished PhD dissertation (Aristotle University of Thessaloniki, 2015).

[18] R. E. Robinson, 'Non-European Foundations of European Imperialism: Sketch for a Theory of Collaboration', in *Studies in the Theory of Imperialism*, ed. Roger Owen and Robert B. Sutcliffe (London: Longman, 1972), 117–42, 120–21.

perceived his actions. His relationship with the British and his willingness to work with them triggered the hatred of the pro-*enosis* far right that seemingly led to his assassination. The book also explores the role of the far right and far left in colonial politics and how the British responded to each. This case study also speaks to the nascent theme of assassinations, the theories associated with them and the significance for violent political groups to control 'their flock'. It is this theory that best indicates that those most likely behind the assassination were far right extremists trying to control the Greek Cypriot political elites from cooperating with the British colonial authorities because they feared that it may have led to a meaningful alternative to *enosis*. To a lesser extent this book explores the existence of a colonial underworld, which contributes to understanding colonial politics and society, and that extremist colonial elites were connected to a criminal underworld.

This monograph adds to recent work on the British Mediterranean. Too often studies focus in isolation on Egypt, Palestine, Cyprus, Malta and Gibraltar without considering each other or the broader British Empire,[19] while work on the British Empire often excludes case studies from the Mediterranean. Although this has improved over the last 12 years,[20] much more work is needed to integrate the entire colonial experience. This is important to highlight their worth to and place in the British Empire, and to show that their experiences were reflections of the Empire: that the story of the British Empire features similarities and differences across themes and geographies, to form, as Ballantyne argues, 'webs of Empire'.[21] In isolation, the assassination of Triantafyllides is a rarity in the British Empire, yet the broader picture of national liberation politics and colonial cooperation to achieve 'decolonisation' is not.

There is a long and current debate in colonial history on the nature and degree of evasion, protest, resistance and rebellion on the one hand, and cooperation and collaboration on the other. The first historian to write seriously about colonial cooperation was Ronald Robinson in his 1972 article on the co-option of local elite by the imperial power, in which he makes subtle distinctions between collaboration and cooperation.[22] More recently Antoinette Burton has argued that colonial subjects protested, resisted and

---

[19] Research does not need to be comparative to do this, it merely needs to be situated in the broader imperial context, which many books, especially on Cyprus, do not do, preferring to situate them alongside the histories of Greece and Turkey, the two supposed 'motherlands', thus accepting the nationalism from the minority of educated classes.
[20] This has been my aim with my first three monographs and also that of numerous other publications, and the works by Rappas.
[21] Tony Ballantyne, *Webs of Empire: Locating New Zealand's Colonial Past* (Wellington: Bridget Williams Books, 2012).
[22] Robinson, 'Non-European Foundations of European Imperialism', 120–21.

rebelled against colonial authority.²³ The problem is the conflation of cooperation and collaboration, because collaboration has negative connotations, and there is a failure to view cooperation as a legitimate method to serve liberation. Katsourides stated that Cypriot elites working with the British to bring about liberation/ decolonisation was 'strange' and 'unusual', a judgement based on anti-colonial politics and memory, since it was normal throughout the British Empire, especially Malta.²⁴ The same author, along with Alecou, argued that the moderate/centre-right adopted a legal path towards *enosis*, by working with the British, because they were dependent on British rule for their political and economic power.²⁵ This may be true for some, but also true for the pro-*enosis* fanatics who did not want any interim period of self-government as they had been promised and believed they would receive plum state jobs once *enosis* had been achieved.²⁶ There are important differences between those motivated by careerism to work with the British in the colonial administration and those desiring the immediate granting of *enosis* to hopefully be rewarded with jobs in the Greek state: those working with and/or for the British may have been prolonging colonialism, but they were also developing the representative and government institutions of the island, its civic society, as it were, in preparation for a peaceful transition away from colonialism; while those demanding immediate *enosis* knew well that the achievement of their demand meant that Cyprus would import the flawed Greek democracy and party divisions that gripped and divided Greece. As for Triantafyllides, his legal practice not only earned him more money than most Cypriots but the governor too, and a political career would have meant less time to make money as a lawyer. In my view he was not motivated by money, but by the desire to lead.

At the heart of this book is control of the national liberation struggle in Cyprus. Although most of the scholarship has focussed on the national liberation struggle post-1945 and particularly on the 1950s, this book shifts the focus to an earlier period more meaningfully than historians before. While Georghallides captured the hardliners and the moderates and the various pro-*enosis* factions during the 1920s and 1930s, he did not go far enough to

---

²³ Antoinette Burton, *The Trouble with Empire: Challenges to Modern British Imperialism* (Oxford: Oxford University Press, 2015), 12–15.
²⁴ Katsourides, *Greek Cypriot Nationalist Right*, 81.
²⁵ Yiannos Katsourides, 'Anti-Colonial Struggle in Cyprus: Actors, Conceptualisations, Methods and Motives', *Journal of Mediterranean Studies* 23, no. 1 (2014): 31–46; Alexios Alecou, *Communism and Nationalism in Postwar Cyprus, 1945–1955* (New York: Palgrave Macmillan, 2016), 14–16.
²⁶ Varnava, *British Cyprus and the Long Great War*, 103–15; Andrekos Varnava, 'Greek Cypriot "Volunteers" in the Greek Army, 1897–1922: Querying Loyalties and Identity', forthcoming, *Journal of Modern Greek Studies* 38, no. 2 (2020).

explore the differences, particularly in their approaches, or track them to developments in the 1940s and 1950s. Additionally, as his subsequent articles showed, he accepted that *enosis* was a manifestation of the people's will, and thus the nationalist discourses as legitimate.[27] Holland discussed the events of 1931, not to show links with EOKA and the violence adopted or desired by EREK, but to claim that there was a long-standing frustration from pro-*enosis* Cypriots that explained, even mitigated, the violence of EOKA.[28] Rappas and Katsourides were the first to shift the focus of the Cyprus 'problem' from the 1950s to the 1930s, by connecting the various responses (including cooperation) to British rule during this period from Cypriot elites, yet, as stated, Triantafyllides as a politician and his assassination were missing factors.[29]

There was no *enosis* 'movement' as meant by Cypriot national discourse and some historians. Not every Cypriot danced as one to the tune of *enosis*. To be sure it became more played, yet they also became monotonous behind *enosis* and only *enosis*, driven by the handful of individuals, some, as stated above, with a vested interest of being rewarded by the Greek state with government/state jobs after *enosis*: others, true believers, were oblivious to the British and Turkish Cypriot concerns, and the problems facing Cyprus and Greece.[30] Thus I avoid using the word 'movement'. Indeed David French has shown that the *enosis* policy, even during the EOKA years, could not be considered popular given the level of coercion and violence, and the targeting of impressionable youths.[31] In any event, the 'national liberation' struggle in Cyprus, like elsewhere, was a kaleidoscope of differing ideas, involving various personalities, both willing and unwilling to cooperate with the British, who suggested numerous methods, which were often adapted and altered, from the moderate to the extremist, across the ideological spectrum.

---

[27] Georghallides, 'The Cyprus Revolt''; Georghallides, 'Church and State in Cyprus'; Georghallides, 'British Policy on Cyprus'; Georghallides, *A Political and Administrative History of Cyprus*; Georghallides, *Cyprus and the Governorship of Sir Ronald Storrs*.

[28] Robert Holland, *Britain and the Revolt in Cyprus, 1954–1959* (Oxford: Oxford University Press, 1998), 1–19; Robert Holland and Diana Markides, *The British and the Hellenes: Struggles for Mastery in the Eastern Mediterranean 1850–1960* (Oxford: Oxford University Press, 2006), 162–88.

[29] Rappas, *Cyprus in the 1930s*; Alexis Rappas, 'The Cypriot Colonial Civil Servant: Practical Agency through Uncertain Identities', *The Cyprus Review* 18, no. 1 (2006): 121–36; Alexis Rappas, 'The Uncharted World of Cypriot Colonial Servants and the Ideological Foundations of British Rule', *The Cyprus Review* 23, no. 2 (2011): 57–76. Katsourides, *History of the Communist Party in Cyprus*; Katsourides, *Greek Cypriot Nationalist Right*.

[30] Varnava, *British Cyprus and the Long Great War*, 103–15; Varnava, 'Greek Cypriot "Volunteers" in the Greek Army'.

[31] French, *Fighting EOKA*, 64–69, 89–90, 110–11, 159–70, 294–95.

By the 1950s, the two main ideologies dominating the national liberation struggle in Cyprus were the far left communists and the right wing, which was a broader church, consisting of the far right, fascists, pro-Greek Royalists, and conservatives, united by their anti-communism. Ultimately, the bourgeoisie and the industrial and trading classes, which were primarily pro-British, sided with the nationalist right, such as in India, because of their fear of communism threatening their economic and social status.[32]

The Communist Party of Cyprus (CPC), founded in August 1926, was anti-imperialist and opposed *enosis* as a bourgeoise policy. It favoured self-government that would lead to independence, whereby Greek and Turkish Cypriot workers would create a people's republic in a Balkan federation of soviet republics. Communism gained some support as the island diversified from a peasant-agricultural economy and society, with mining and manufacturing industries growing, but the party was heavily suppressed and proscribed after the 1931 disturbances. In 1941 the Left, consisting of centre-left and the far left, formed the Progressive Party of the Working People (AKEL), which adopted self-government as a prelude to *enosis*. It therefore compromised its previous position vis-à-vis the Turkish Cypriots (and smaller demographic minorities) and Cypriot nationalism as expressed through a common homeland and independence, by giving priority to a pro-*enosis* anti-imperialism and Greek nationalism, hoping that one day Cyprus would be a republic in a soviet Greece.[33] It compromised even more when in 1949, now fully under the control of the communists, it adopted *enosis* and only *enosis*, under pressure from the Greek communists. In connection with Triantafyllides, as one prominent Akelist and historian once told me, he was 'a traitor', presumably because (as it was perceived) his cooperation with the British had meant that he was no longer part of the national liberation struggle against British rule.[34] For this reason, and that Triantafyllides was right wing, AKEL and its supports have cared little about his assassination, despite being officially accused in the courts of masterminding it.

On the other hand, the right-wing nationalists were united by their anti-communism. Katsourides showed that the Greek Cypriot nationalist Right emerged before the Great War from the distinctive social classes that had

---

[32] David Lockwood, *The Indian Bourgeoisie: A Political History of the Indian Capitalist Class in the Early Twentieth Century* (London: I.B. Tauris, 2012).

[33] Katsourides, *History of the Communist Party in Cyprus*, 186–95.

[34] Andrekos Varnava, 'An Appraisal of the Works of Rolandos Katsiaounis: Society, Labour and Anti-Colonialism in Cyprus, 1850s-1950s', in *Cypriot Nationalisms in Context: History, Identity, and Politics*, ed. Thekla Kyritsi and Nikos Christofi (Cham, Switzerland: Palgrave Macmillan, 2018), 243–57.

developed and then grew during the interwar years. These socio-political classes belonged to the educated and semi-educated elites, and focussed on the 'old elites' of landowners and traders, including the high-clergy, who were more reliant on the British (as they had been on the Ottomans) for their livelihoods and status, and the 'new elites' of white-collar professionals, including some clergy, and a more volatile bourgeoisie.[35] In reality there existed four right-wing camps: the intransigent far right, firstly EREK and then from 1946 the 'X Organisation', who wanted *enosis* so Cyprus could be a right-wing dictatorship under the control of Greece and thus stave off communism, socialism and liberalism; a right-wing conservative group under Dervis that blew with the wind, as it were, since before 1939 his power derived from his close relationship with the governor, Sir Herbert Richmond Palmer, but this waned during the war, and so he turned to forming a right-wing party (KEK), which became closely aligned with the 'X Organisation'; a pro-church nationalist right wing, represented by Archbishop Leontios, that was less intransigent when it came to *enosis* and only *enosis*, and was willing to accept a constitutional path to *enosis* as well as working with all ideological forces, including the communists; and a fourth group, mainly of professionals, who believed that the only path to *enosis* was the constitutional path, in which the Cypriot people would develop strong liberal democratic institutions before achieving liberation. The far right Cypriot nationalists, who emerged in the late 1920s and were uncompromising in their *enosis* stance, were instrumental in the violent disturbances in October 1931; they were also the initial prime suspects in the assassination of Triantafyllides and brought Greek Civil War politics to Cyprus after the Second World War, soon after they formed EOKA and essentially took the entire Right and Cyprus over the abyss.

As previously stated, ownership and control of the national liberation struggle is at the heart of this book. In 2007 Rolandos Katsiaounis penned a largely ignored yet significant article, which argued that the formation of EOKA was motivated just as much by the desire to control the direction of the national liberation struggle and shutting the left wing out as it was about *enosis* and being anti-imperial.[36] Sia Anagnostopoulou agreed.[37] It was true that the Right believed that the British would grant *enosis* as part of an anti-communist alliance with Greece and that the far right aimed to control the national liberation struggle and take the right wing and centre-right with it,

---

[35] Katsourides, *Greek Cypriot Nationalist Right*.
[36] Rolandos Katsiaounis, 'Cyprus 1931–1959: The Politics of the Anti-Colonial Movement', *Annual of the Cyprus Research Centre* (2007): 441–69.
[37] Sia Anagnostopoulou, 'Makarios III, 1950–77: Creating the Ethnarchic State', in Varnava and Michael (eds), *The Archbishops of Cyprus in the Modern Age*, 240–92.

and, of course, shut out the Left. As they pointed out, their main method of doing this was to form EOKA, which used sabotage, guerrilla warfare and targeted assassination to achieve *enosis*. These methods are integral to most terrorist organisations. One may argue that 'one man's terrorist is another man's freedom fighter' and for many Greek Cypriots EOKA members were 'freedom fighters', yet for many others they were 'terrorists'. Yet EOKA, as well as the Turkish Resistance Organisation (TMT – *Türk Mukavemet Teşkilatı*) for the Turkish Cypriots (formed to combat EOKA) and the British state response (which included torture), all fit the label of terrorism. A fundamental characteristic of terrorist group activity is the use of violence to control 'their own flock', as it were, the community they claim to represent.[38] This was no less the case with EOKA, which, as previously mentioned, killed more Greek Cypriots than British and Turkish Cypriots put together. But the use of coercion and even violence is not limited to an active terrorist group. In Europe in the 1930s, both the far left (communist) and far right (fascist etc.), implemented several violent purges and used violence against opponents, including assassinations and assassination attempts (with several on Venizelos).[39]

And the fundamental characteristic of such purges or assassinations is that the ringleaders did not pull the trigger, but used loyal subordinates or paid assassins. This leads to the under-researched fields of the colonial underworld and assassinations. Indeed, Triantafyllides is one of only two nationalist leaders assassinated by members of their own community and former allies during British rule: the other, Aung San, was assassinated only six months before Burmese independence.[40] As will be shown, Triantafyllides was probably assassinated on the order of his former nationalist associates.[41] He was seen by those who seemingly had him assassinated as a 'British lackey', so comparisons

---

[38] A. P. Schmid and A. J. Jongman, *Political Terrorism: A New Guide to Actors, Authors, Concepts, Data Bases, Theories, and Literature* (Amsterdam: North-Holland, 1988).

[39] Robert Gellately, *Lenin, Stalin, and Hitler: The Age of Social Catastrophe* (New York: Knopf, 2007); George Mavrogordatos, *Stillborn Republic: Social Coalitions and Party Strategies in Greece, 1922–1936* (Berkeley: University of California Press, 1983), 46, 48, 62, 241.

[40] Justin Wintle, *Perfect Hostage: A Life of Aung San Suu Kyi, Burma's Prisoner of Conscience* (New York: Skyhorse, 2007).

[41] Another example was Michael Collins, killed by anti-Treaty Irish nationalists in 1922, but this was after the Anglo-Irish Treaty of December 1921 and thus during the transition from British to Irish rule. See S. M. Sigerson, *The Assassination of Michael Collins* (Createspace, 2013). Another example was the failed attempt to kill Lord Strickland in Malta in 1930. Although not a nationalist, he was considered pro-British. Henry Frendo, *Europe and Empire: Culture, Politics and Identity in Malta and the Mediterranean (1912–1946)* (Malta: Midsea, 2012), 231. The case of Mahatma Gandhi is different, since he was assassinated by a Hindu nationalist in the postcolonial period and blaming him for partition.

can be made with imperial assassinations. Ball's article on the assassination culture of imperial Britain, focussing on the assassination of leading British figures by colonials, offers some comparison on whether imperial politics is more prone to assassinations than metropolitan politics and British anxiety in reacting to them.[42]

Political science literature claims that imperial polities were more prone to assassinations because the colonial executive was weak numerically, exclusively consisted of British officials and repression was inherent in the imperial system, engendering violent responses from the colonised.[43] Yet the majority of the local elites in the British Empire were well-educated and owed their education and sometimes careers to British rule. In Cyprus, British rule was more liberal than Ottoman rule, while the alternatives, *enosis* or a return to Ottoman/Turkish rule, were no more democratic, since both Greece and Turkey suffered from democratic deficits during the interwar years.[44] Ball also discusses the British anxiety in responding to these assassinations and how the standard British response originated with the assassination of Sir Curzon Wyllie, previously the aide-de-camp of the Secretary of State for India, Lord George Hamilton, in 1909 and took the form of (a) arguing that there was an organised conspiracy; (b) that only a few people were behind it; and (c) that the conspiracy was serious because it was violent, not because it could repeat itself.[45] The British authorities believed that Triantafyllides's assassination was an organised conspiracy of the few (initially from the far right, but then from the far left), yet initially believed more would follow, a view that seemingly changed within six months.

Those behind Triantafyllides's assassination, whether from the far right or far left, were educated men with means (especially from the Right), who paid a Cypriot underworld figure to do it. This is the first study to mention the Cypriot underworld during the colonial period. Little has been published on colonial underworlds in the twentieth century beyond Ireland and Singapore.[46] Both these resemble Cyprus, since Irish republicans employed political assassination, while the Singaporean secret societies were connected to political

---

[42] Simon Ball, 'The Assassination Culture of Imperial Britain, 1909–1979', *The Historical Journal* 56, no. 1 (2013): 231–56.

[43] Ibid., 234.

[44] Thomas Gallant, *Modern Greece: From the War of Independence to the Present* (London: Bloomsbury, 2016), 189–220. Erik Zürcher, *The Young Turk Legacy and Nation Building: From the Ottoman Empire to Atatürk's Turkey* (London: I.B. Tauris, 2010).

[45] Ball, 'The Assassination Culture'.

[46] For the previous century see, Kirsten McKenzie, *Imperial Underworld: An Escaped Convict and the Transformation of the British Colonial Order* (Cambridge: Cambridge University Press, 2016).

elites involved in clandestine activities.[47] What was colonial about them was their growth under a colonial system in which colonial rule and responses to it offered opportunities for criminality, including political crime. This subject cannot be fully explored here because the sources do not allow it and it would detract from the main aim of exploring who was behind the assassination of Triantafyllides.

Finally, it is important to clarify that this is not a biography, although inevitably given the focus, it is biographical. Often biographies become hagiographies, when authors become too close to their subjects. This monograph is not that, yet it does balance the record. I had no preconceived ideas about who was responsible. My analysis is built upon the sources, reading them both with and against the grain, and on my years spent understanding Cypriot history. Yet, I cannot shy from my view that as a political intellectual, Triantafyllides was ahead of his time in arguing that *enosis* or liberation could only be achieved with British consent, which would come once the Cypriots had developed economically, socially and politically (strong democratic foundations). Meanwhile, the pro-*enosis* far right led Cyprus off the abyss with their maximalist stance on *enosis* and efforts to import Greek far right control in Cyprus.

Methodology

It is possible to investigate the assassination of Triantafyllides only after creating a 'community of records'. The assassination offers insights for the debate on the value of the 'colonial archive', given that it is created by the colonial agents of imperial power, all-powerful white men, reporting to their superiors on the colonised societies they administered and controlled.

Stoler established how and why the colonial archive was a consequential act of colonialism. She argued that scholars needed to treat the colonial archive as one archive to add to others, namely of local creation, to create a new composite colonial archive (in line with the arguments of Jean and John Comaroff);[48] and as an account of the subjective knowledge created by the colonial authorities. Thus the colonial archive needed subjecting to a further

---

[47] Tom Bowden, 'The Irish Underworld and the War of Independence 1919–21', *Journal of Contemporary History* 8, no. 2 (1973): 3–23; Kamaludeen Mohamed Nasir, 'Protected Sites: Reconceptualising Secret Societies in Colonial and Postcolonial Singapore', *Journal of Historical Sociology* 29, no. 2 (2016): 232–49.

[48] See Jean and John Comaroff, *Ethnography and the Historical Imagination* (Boulder: Westview Press, 1992).

critical scrutiny, both against and with the grain.[49] Jeannette Bastian argued for an expanded notion of the archive to include all material remains and oral evidence to create a 'community of records'.[50] Burton agreed, challenging the positivist view of history that accepted the objectivity of written official sources over the subjectivity of local unofficial ones.[51]

The methodology is to read the archive as a collection of subjective evidence – 'community of records' – that requires understanding the broader context of those records, their origin and authors. The records are read with the grain, understood as reading to understand the perspective of the author, *and* against the grain, reading to seek out the contradictions, silences and faulty logic of the author. Of course, this is what all historians should be doing, but how many do for every document? Also, in this instance, the British authorities have seemingly read some of the evidence with and not against the grain, and thus come to wrong conclusions, evidenced by the court rejecting their communist conspiracy theory.

Using local sources to create a 'community of records' is necessary to reconstruct the past and offers an opportunity to reinterpret, especially against the grain, the available official data gathered by the British. The use of both local (Cypriot) and regional (Greek) newspapers informed and propagated nationalist politics, as argued more broadly by Anderson.[52] Although here the 'community of records' is incomplete, the missing archive and newspapers, and redacted files, does not hinder the investigation, because a large community of records was formed.

There is a growing literature on 'Operation Legacy', the British policy to destroy or remove sensitive files from the colonies upon their withdrawal, the result of which was the 'migrated files' acknowledged in 2011.[53] As Sato has

---

[49] Ann Laura Stoler, 'Colonial Archives and the Arts of Governance', *Archival Science* 2 (2002): 87–109; Ann Laura Stoler, *Along the Archival Grain: Epistemic Anxieties and Colonial Common Sense* (Princeton: Princeton University Press, 2010).

[50] Jeannette Allis Bastian, 'Reading Colonial Records through an Archival Lens: The Provenance of Place, Space and Creation', *Archival Science* 6 (2006): 267–84.

[51] Antoinette Burton (ed.), *Archive Stories: Facts, Fictions, and the Writing of History* (Durham: Duke University Press, 2005).

[52] Benedict Anderson, *Imagined Communities* (London: Verso, 1983).

[53] David M. Anderson, 'Mau Mau in the High Court and the "Lost" British Empire Archives: Colonial Conspiracy or Bureaucratic Bungle?', *The Journal of Imperial and Commonwealth History* 39, no. 5 (2011): 699–716; Mandy Banton, ' "Lost" and "Found": The Concealment and Release of the Foreign and Commonwealth Office "Migrated Archives" ', *Comma* 2012, no. 1 (2012): 33–46; Mandy Banton, 'Destroy? "Migrate"? Conceal? British Strategies for the Disposal of Sensitive Records of Colonial Administrations at Independence', *The Journal of Imperial and Commonwealth History* 40, no. 2 (2012): 321–35.

argued, the literature engenders many possible enquiries within and outside the British Empire, and this study is the first to discuss Cyprus.[54] Thus far the literature has assumed or implied that almost all the files removed were on decolonisation, which is untrue, as this book shows. This study was not hindered by the extracted or redacted documents, which were eventually released from the files held at the National Archives of the UK. There are three files in the National Archives of the UK on the assassination: FCO141/2497, CO67/253/10 and CO67/253/11. The two Colonial Office files were previously released without any documents retained or redacted. A passage initially redacted in FCO141/2497 was not redacted in CO67/253/11. The document, a letter (30 January 1934) by Theophanis Theodotou to the Secretary of State for the Colonies, contains the redacted passage referring to Zenon Severis, the nephew of Theodotou's wife (daughter of Christodoulos Severis), informing him that completed personal insurance forms were found in Triantafyllides's office, indicating that he had feared assassination after receiving threatening letters. Severis had nothing to do with the crime, while the names that Theodotou linked to the assassination were not redacted. This brings into question the redacting process and the value of redacted passages and extracted pages. Having said this, when the process is so thorough, as it is for communist files in relation to Cyprus, the retention and redacting process cannot but be considered a hindrance to uncovering the historical record.

Also, the investigation was not hindered by missing archival material. The missing colonial court archives, burnt a few years ago by the Greek Cypriot authorities,[55] would have been handy, but proved unnecessary since the court proceedings were reported in detail in the local newspapers. Then there was the newspaper that Triantafyllides reputedly published, *Εμπρός* (Forward).[56] This is a more mysterious disappearance. None of the places holding newspaper archives in Cyprus, both north and south of the divide, had copies, although they acknowledged that it had existed. The family could not help either.[57] Obviously, if it had been possible to have more of his own words it

---

[54] Shohei Sata, '"Operation Legacy": Britain's Destruction and Concealment of Colonial Records Worldwide', *The Journal of Imperial and Commonwealth History* 45, no. 4 (2017): 1–23, 16.

[55] This is based on conversations with Greek Cypriot legal experts. Turkish Cypriot legal experts have suggested that the records might be in the Turkish Cypriot court house, but after several searches nothing was found.

[56] Aristedis Coudounaris, *Βιογραφικόν Λεξικόν Κυπρίων, 1800–1920* [Biographical Lexicon of Cypriots, 1800–1920] (Nicosia, 2001), 371–72.

[57] FCO141/2501, on *Embros* from 1934–37, contained nothing on Triantafyllides, covering the period after his death.

would have been better, yet what is available is telling, including views from others. Additionally, the lack of newspaper coverage of the earlier conviction of Stavros Christodoulou for attempted murder may have been a setback, since it would have been interesting to see if there were any allegations as to who may have paid him.

Generally autobiographies/memoirs provide an insight into the intimate thoughts and relations of the authors, and the information and justification behind their actions. Obviously, they can leave much out, but in the case of Greek Cypriot right-wing extremists, as they are considered heroes for their roles in the events of 1931 and EOKA, they openly discuss almost everything associated with their activities. The autobiography of Savvas Loizides, a leading pro-*enosis* fanatic from the late 1920s, was particularly important, although another by his friend and associate, Theophanis Tsangarides, proved to be of limited use.[58] British autobiographies were less significant. Both Sir Ronald Storrs, the Governor of Cyprus from 1926 to 32, who often played chess with Triantafyllides, and the secretary of state for the Colonies, Philip Cunliffe-Lister, who had met Triantafyllides, wrote detailed memoirs that did not mention Triantafyllides or his assassination.[59] Yet the diary and private papers of Sir Henry Blackall, the Attorney General, proved invaluable.

Finally, within this 'community of records', unofficial oral sources, namely unsubstantiated rumours, exist. These will not form the basis of the evidence scrutinised, but must be addressed because some are seemingly connected to the efforts at the time to divert attention from a political murder (assassination) to a personal one. When discussing these rumours, I have remained respectful to the Triantafyllides family.

These rumours refer to two motives for the shooting of Triantafyllides, personal or political. The personal motives claim that Triantafyllides had led 'an immoral life', which included accusations of heterosexual and homosexual liaisons. The most popular theory to account for his shooting that I heard was '*γυναικοδουλειές*' (i.e., 'women's business'). In 2018, I visited the Crime Investigation Department in Nicosia and the officer responsible for my case was interested in my research, calling a relative who had been the bodyguard

---

[58] Savvas Loizides, *Άτυχη Κύπρος: Πως Έζησα τους Πόθους και τους Καημούς της 1910–1980* [Luckless Cyprus: How I Lived through Its Desires and Sorrows 1910–1980] (Athens: Bergade, 1980); Theophanis Tsangarides, *Το Ημερολόγιον ενος Εξόριστου* [The Diary of an Exile] (Athens, 1948).

[59] Sir Ronald Storrs, *Orientations* (London: Readers Union, 1939); Viscount Swinton (Cunliffe-Lister), *I Remember* (London: Hutchinson, 1948).

for Michalakis Triantafyllides when he had been Attorney General. I heard (he was on speaker phone) his response to the motives as 'γυναικοδουλειές'. He had either never spoken to Michalakis Triantafyllides about what he knew, or did not believe it, indicating how ingrained the personal motive theory is. One problem with this theory, as the evidence will show, is that it originates at the time of his death from his enemies in Athens, who clearly wanted to deflect attention away from the theory of assassination after their colleagues had been interned in Cyprus on suspicion of involvement. Another problem is that having sexual liaisons is hardly unusual in most societies and certainly not in Cyprus, where sexual promiscuity was one cause for the high incidence of venereal diseases.[60] If every man was killed for having an affair, there would have been many other high-profile murders and murder attempts. Additionally, the murder of elites in Cyprus was rare and crimes of passion usually occurred in rural communities and by the jilted party in a fit of rage, not by hiring someone.[61]

As regards the political motives rumoured to have been behind the assassination, these are more trustworthy. The rumours do not include a communist conspiracy and revolve around Triantafyllides being silenced by right-wing extremists opposed to his cooperation with the British. This was said to me several times and also to my research assistant working in the Public Information Office newspaper archive by a woman researching her family tree. But the most credible source came from someone related to the Triantafyllides family, who revealed that he had been told that Michalakis Triantafyllides, while on a visit to London, had been approached by a man asking to see him privately, where he revealed that he was the assassin and had been paid £100 by Bishop Makarios of Kyrenia. This partly matches what Michalakis stated in his 2002 interview and the evidence and interpretation presented in this monograph.

These rumours and information take the story into the field of public and private historical memory. This is important in exploring who was behind the assassination and understanding why it has been silenced or distorted in the historiography and historical consciousness. This is not the first time that I have explored such silences in Cypriot history, such as in connection with the Cypriot Mule Corps during the Great War.[62] For that there was a vast

---

[60] Andrekos Varnava, 'The Origins and Prevalence of and Campaigns to Eradicate Venereal Diseases in British Colonial Cyprus, 1916–1939', *Social History of Medicine* 33, no. 1 (2020): 173–200.

[61] John G. Peristiany, *Honour and Shame: The Values of Mediterranean Society* (Chicago: University of Chicago Press, 1966); Vassos Argyrou, *Tradition and Modernity in the Mediterranean: The Wedding as Symbolic Struggle* (Cambridge: Cambridge University Press, 1996).

[62] Andrekos Varnava, 'The Politics of Forgetting the Cypriot Mule Corps', in *The Great War and the British Empire: Culture and Society*, ed. Michael J. K. Walsh and Andrekos

literature on war memory and forgetting. But this is not the case for assassination literature. One can appreciate silences and distortions over assassinations in high-profile circumstances, such as Michael Collins, John F. Kennedy, Robert F. Kennedy, Martin Luther King Jr and Malcolm X. When you add cold case to the dynamic of assassination the levels of silence and distortion increase, especially when the plotters were prominent in society. Not only are there no other comparable cases within the British imperial context like this assassination but there are also few if any cases of unsolved assassination, which have been silenced from the historical record and public consciousness either. While one could list numerous unsolved assassinations, those cases, unlike Triantafyllides, have increased public curiosity and their legacy grows amongst supporters. Yet, Triantafyllides has few supporters. In a country which lauds its EOKA and nationalist extremists by naming streets, schools and airports after them, and erecting statues of them, Triantafyllides has been completely expunged from historical consciousness by the *Eokatokratia*[63] that developed in the postcolonial period and which continues to frame the state. And that is how his enemies like it. He was considered a traitor for cooperating with the British, though not the only one, but the one to lose his life for it, so his story had to be silenced or distorted.

The book is structured into four main chapters. The first provides the necessary background on Cyprus and the politics and public service of Triantafyllides before his assassination. It particularly focuses upon the divisions within Cypriot politics and relations between the British authorities and Cypriots in public life. It aims to show that there was a wide range of Cypriot responses to British colonialism and that the dominant discourse of opposition and demand for *enosis* was only one and not the most dominant, although the loudest. The chapter tracks how the extremists and Triantafyllides went in opposite directions, with the fanatics planning to antagonise the British into granting *enosis*, and Triantafyllides believing in practical and flexible approaches, and that the best way was to win over the British by developing the Cypriots to be able to support a liberation movement. The events of 1931 and the British crackdown are explored in so far as these impacted on the discussion connected to Triantafyllides. The chapter ends with the formation of the advisory council and how his acceptance to join it triggered a far right backlash.

Varnava (London: Routledge, 2017), 291–303; Varnava, *Serving the Empire in the Great War*, 210–26.

[63] This is a play on the term *Τουρκοκρατία/Turcokratia* (held by the Turks) and *Αγγλοκρατία/Anglokratia* (held by the English), which are commonly used by Cypriot and Greek historians of Cyprus and the public in general.

Chapters 2 and 3 are the guts of the book, where the cold case is explored. They are divided, unusually perhaps, by methodology. Chapter 2 primarily explores the case from the public discourses in Cyprus at the time, namely through the newspapers. These illuminate two periods of the Triantafyllides case. The first on the shooting, his death and the funeral and memorial services, which provide the reactions from the newspaper editors, the public and Triantafyllides's friends and colleagues. Additionally, and most importantly, the articles also establish a timeline of the before and after the shooting, until his death, which help in analysing the second series of articles, on the legal proceedings against Stavros Christodoulou, a year after the assassination. Without the court records or account of the proceedings in the government files, the extensive detail of the court case in the newspapers proved essential.

Chapter 3 primarily explores the case using the colonial archive and otherwise 'hidden' sources revealed only by the colonial archive, such as newspapers in Greece. This allows for an understanding of the evidence the British authorities had, and for how they read it. It also allows for an understanding of the gaps in their evidence and criticism of their analysis and actions. The records go beyond these Colonial Office and Foreign and Commonwealth Office files that mention Triantafyllides in their title; to include Foreign Office files and private papers and diaries. Here the community of records is further expanded to include Greek newspapers, which the British only read with the grain. The chapter also explores the possibility of a British conspiracy to cover up and deflect blame away from the far right right-wing nationalists. This is one of the gaps in the information provided by Michalakis Triantafyllides: if the British had a file and knew that those responsible were far right fanatics from Kyrenia, why did they pursue a communist conspiracy theory?

The last of the main chapters explores how the men who seemingly plotted the assassination had a long history of political violence, which pre-and-post-dates the assassination, and helps to understand how it has been remembered and forgotten. This involves discussing the Cyprus 'problem', the control exerted in Cyprus over the historical record and consciousness, and how this has been difficult, until more recently, to overcome in order to present the historical record dispassionately. The chapter shows that those seemingly behind the assassination later formed EOKA and were possibly linked to the mysterious deaths of Dr Angelos Zemenides in London in 1933 and Archbishop Leontios in Cyprus in 1947. This chapter shows a link between the disinformation associated with the assassination and the control exerted over historical memory and historiography by the state controlling the national narrative of postcolonial Cyprus.

The conclusion summarises the findings, presenting them methodically to support the theory of who were behind the assassination of Triantafyllides. It presents the broader significance of the story to historical methodology and the historiographies of the British Empire and Cyprus. It then explores how the tragic assassination of Triantafyllides had consequences for the political development of Cyprus and for a divided Cyprus today. It even asks the hypothetical question: What could Cyprus have been like had Triantafyllides not been assassinated?

What follows is a theory on who masterminded the assassination of Triantafyllides. This is not about reopening the case or the theory standing up in court. This is a historical investigation. All historical work reconstructs the past based on the evidence available. This is no different. There were no preconceived views, despite the rumours and disclosures. I am motivated not merely to search for 'the truth', but to achieve closure for Cypriots divided by the violence that gripped their island in the 1950s and led to partition, first in 1963 and more completely in 1974. Pro-*enosis* violence seemingly dates to the ruthless and bloody conspiracy to assassinate a man who had, as had many others, a different method by which to achieve *enosis* or liberation. The idea that Cypriots must develop economically, socially and politically may have successfully led to *enosis* or a more feasible alternative, which did not violently displace Cypriots. But that was what the plotters most feared.

Chapter 1
TRIANTAFYLLIDES BEFORE HIS ASSASSINATION

> Politics, like it is said, is the art of pursuing the possible. Politics is intelligent and creative adaptation to situations.
> Antonios Triantafyllides, *Ελευθερία*, 8 November 1933, 2.

Antonios (often Antonakis) Triantafyllides was born on 26 January 1890 to a Cypriot family with prominent and significant public service dating from the late Ottoman period and his family became prominent Cypriots too. His father was Michalakis and his grandfather, and namesake, born in Beirut, had been instrumental in removing Archbishop Panaretos for abuse of power in 1840 and was a member of deputations to Constantinople (1840, 1856 and 1870), with that in 1856 obtaining administrative reforms from the Porte.[1] Antonakis was educated in Nicosia, studied law at the University of Athens (1907–11) and returned to Nicosia and established in July 1912 what became one of the finest law firms in Cyprus.[2]

His three sons were all prominent Cypriots. His eldest, Michalakis (1927–2005), had represented EOKA members before the courts, and was considered, even at 28 when EOKA started by Charles Foley, a British journalist sympathetic to EOKA, as 'one of the most brilliant lawyers' in Cyprus.[3] Michalakis was a member of the Constitutional Commission (1959–60) that drew up the constitution, was appointed judge of the Supreme Constitutional Court when Cyprus became independent in 1960, was made a judge of the Supreme Court in 1964, before being appointed president of the Supreme Court in 1971 and Attorney General in 1988 by President George Vassiliou

---

[1] *Πάφος* (*Paphos*), 19 January 1934, 1; Coudounaris, *Βιογραφικόν Λεξικόν Κυπρίων*, 371; Michalis N. Michael, 'Panaretos, 1827–1840: His Struggle for Absolute Power during the Era of Ottoman Administrative Reforms', in Varnava and Michael (eds), *The Archbishops of Cyprus in the Modern Age*, 69–87, 72, 86.
[2] *Πρωινή* (Morning), 14 January 1934, 4.
[3] Charles Foley, *Island in Revolt* (London: Longmans 1962), 146.

and his successor, President Glafkos Clerides, until Michalakis retired in 1995.[4] In 1974, when the Greek Junta ordered the coup against President Archbishop Makarios III, Nicos Sampson, a former EOKA gunman and later paramilitary leader, who became the president of the coup, was ordered to find Michalakis Triantafyllides to be the president. Triantafyllides was overseas, but is unlikely to have accepted, since the Junta wanted him only to give legitimacy to the coup.[5] His second son, Solon (b. 1932; d. 2016), was an accountant, the first president of the Institute of Certified Public Accountants of Cyprus in 1961, and the long-time chairman of the Bank of Cyprus, 1988–2005 (Antonios was on the board when he died). During his chairmanship, the Bank of Cyprus grew, he invested more in its Cultural Foundation, and established the Bank of Cyprus Oncology Centre.[6] And Antonios's third son, Antis (b. 1933), started one of the largest and most successful law firms in the island in 1955, and was highly recommended as a constitutional lawyer by Blackall, the Attorney General (1932–36), when his father was assassinated in the 1960s.[7] Many of Antonios Triantafyllides's grandchildren are prominent Cypriots. Of these, two children of Michalakis stand out. Christos M. Triantafyllides is a prominent lawyer, former president of the Cyprus Football Association and the right-wing APOEL football club in Nicosia (as had been his father, 1967–68), and has served on the Appeal Board of FIFA. Currently, he is on the committee advising the president of the Republic in the intercommunal talks. His sister, Stella Kyriakides, has perhaps been even more prominent. She was a successful clinical child psychologist in the Ministry of Health (1976–2006) before entering politics. Since 2013 she has been the vice-president of the neoliberal-conservative Democratic Rally, served (as the first Cypriot and third woman) as president of the Parliamentary Assembly of the Council of Europe (2017–18) and in 2019 became the European Commissioner for Health and Food Safety.

Antonios Triantafyllides became politically active as soon as he returned to Cyprus in 1912. In that year the Balkan War raged and a small group of educated Cypriots wanted to contribute, either as volunteers (there were

---

[4] Michalakis Triantafyllides interview, 1 February 2002, in Solomonidou-Drousiotou, *Η Ζωή μου σε Πρώτο Πρόσωπο*, 33–41.
[5] Makarios Drousiotis, *Cyprus 1974: Greek Coup and Turkish Invasion* (Mannheim und Mohnesee: Bibliopolis, 2006), 172, 181–82; Jan Asmussen, *Cyprus at War: Diplomacy and Conflict during the 1974 Crisis* (London: I.B. Tauris, 2008), 234.
[6] Nadina Pafitou, *Bank of Cyprus Chronicle, 1899–2009* (Nicosia: Bank of Cyprus, 2010), 37.
[7] MSS Brit Emp s447, papers of Sir Henry William Blackall (hereafter 'Blackall Papers'), Blackall to Thompson, 26 October 1963. Blackall married Maria Severis, daughter of Demosthenis Severis and sister of Zenon, in 1934 and lived in Cyprus after his retirement.

only about 1,500) or for fundraising.[8] Triantafyllides made his first political intervention by organising and leading the 'young professionals', a group of recently graduated lawyers, doctors and other professionals, who wanted to professionalise the fundraising campaign, and attacked the older generation of politicians, whether it was the traditional landowner and moderate, Paschalis Constantinides, or the Greek-born firebrand nationalist, Nicholas Katalanos, for being yesterday's men.[9] Then in 1914 Triantafyllides was elected to the municipal council in Nicosia and started writing a regular column for *Ελευθερία* (Freedom) titled 'From Life', with perceptive and witty observations on politics and society, and in 1917 and 1918 a serialised fictional narrative with relevance to society under the pseudonym "*Μαρία η Συγκλητική*" (Maria was a 16th- century historical figure).[10] By 1916 Triantafyllides had regular contact with Venizelos, the Greek prime minister (who had in 1916 established a pro-Entente government in Salonica opposed to the neutrality of King Constantine) to align his stance on *enosis* with Venizelos.[11] By 1920 he was well known for his commentary on politics, government and society in Cyprus, including on the Armenian refugee crisis.[12] His national profile grew in 1920 when he acted as the private secretary to Archbishop Kyrillos III during the Greek Cypriot deputation to London.[13] This deputation followed the failed one in 1919 in demanding *enosis*.[14] Kyrillos and Triantafyllides met Venizelos in Paris and he expressed his optimism about achieving *enosis* through winning British and Turkish Cypriot acceptance.[15] This meeting was pivotal for Triantafyllides as he became a lifelong friend of Venizelos and adopted his view on *enosis*, at least by 1931. The deputation failed and its supporters, Triantafyllides included, formed the 'political organisation' in 1921, in an

---

[8] CO67/176/16873, telegram, Clauson to Harcourt, 10 April 1915. Papapolyviou accepts Clauson's estimate. Petros Papapolyviou, *Η Κύπρος και οι Βαλκανικοί Πόλεμοι: Συμβολή στην Ιστορία του Κυπριακού Εθελοντισμού* [Cyprus and the Balkan Wars: Contribution to the History of Cypriot Volunteerism] (Nicosia: Cyprus Research Centre, 1997), 228.

[9] Papapolyviou, *Η Κύπρος και οι Βαλκανικοί Πόλεμοι*, 106–7.

[10] *Private Papers of Stelios A. Triantafyllides*, Nicosia, Cyprus.

[11] Ibid., Triantafyllides to Venizelos, 18 September 1916; Venizelos to Triantafyllides, 16 November 1916.

[12] *Πρωινή*, 18 January 1934, 1; *Πάφος*, 19 January 1934, 1. Also see *Private Papers of Stelios A. Triantafyllides*, Nicosia, Cyprus.

[13] *Ώρα* (Time), 15 January 1934, 4; *Φωνή της Κύπρου* (Voice of Cyprus), 20 January 1934, 2.

[14] Varnava, *British Cyprus and the Long Great War*, 155–217.

[15] *Ελευθερία*, 20 March 1920; *Ελευθερία*, 17 April 1920; *Ελευθερία*, 1 May 1920 (for Triantafyllides's account). Georghallides, *A Political and Administrative History of Cyprus*, 146–47. Venizelos promised the Cypriot Muslims administrative positions in both Cyprus and the new Greek territories.

Figure 1.1 Photo of Antonios Triantafyllides in 1919, J.P. Foscolo Studio.
Source: Courtesy of Dr Nicholas Coureas, Nicosia, Cyprus.

attempt by the nationalist elites to form a loose pro-*enosis* party, to continue the *enosis* struggle despite the British rejection (Figure 1.1).[16]

Along with Neoptolemos Paschalis (son of Paschalis Constantinides), Triantafyllides represented the new generation of young professionals in the 'political organisation', offering a more sophisticated and flexible alternative to Theophanis Theodotou and the fanatical Bishop of Kyrenia, Makarios. Theodotou, who became Triantafyllides's father-in-law, had been a long-time firebrand, who had earned the wrath of the British authorities with his efforts to stamp out opposition to *enosis* or any intermediate approach, and with his irresponsible activities which the British feared might lead to violent clashes between Greek and Turkish Cypriots. Makarios was even more extreme in condemning any back down from *enosis*. Both were most

---

[16] Georghallides, *A Political and Administrative History of Cyprus*, 146–66, 215–20; Varnava, *British Cyprus and the Long Great War*, 155–217.

disliked by the British as unrepentant supporters of King Constantine, who had kept Greece neutral until his abdication in 1917. Triantafyllides, on the other hand, as a Venizelist liberal, wanted a more professional prosecution of *enosis*, and was one of the six (including Ioannis Clerides, another leading advocate) to draft the regulations of the 'political organisation'. In October 1921, Triantafyllides, in supporting Paschalis's call for a boycott of the elections to the legislative council, criticised the members of the legislative council and others willing to work with the British, even for maintaining social relations with them, because this was not a true 'opposition policy'. Their proposal was adopted with the support of others, including Dr Miltiades Coureas, George Markides, Dr Ioannis Pigasiou and George Hadji Pavlou.[17]

Thus, Triantafyllides's profile grew, so much that – as he publicly revealed in *Ελευθερία* in 1929 – the British authorities offered through him a new constitution in December 1921. This would have included a legislative council with a Greek Cypriot majority, control of finances, Cypriots appointed to government positions, and an undertaking to prepare the island for a 'Maltese style' constitution. In exchange the British wanted the boycott policy abandoned. Triantafyllides hinted at a possible constitutional offer, which might be accepted if *enosis* could be envisaged, but the 'national council', the main body of the 'political organisation', maintained the boycott policy.[18]

By the autumn of 1922, Sir Malcolm Stevenson, the High Commissioner, believed that the 'political organisation' was 'moribund' and that there was widespread dissatisfaction with the boycott of the elections for the legislative council in 1922. Consequently, at the 'national council' meetings on 2 and 3 December 1922, Triantafyllides proposed a resolution, which was passed, to pursue constitutional liberties as a prelude to *enosis*, supported by Ioannis Clerides, who wanted a 'Maltese type' constitution, and seemingly knew of the British offer made via Triantafyllides a year earlier.[19] But by 4 September 1923 the 'national council' had acknowledged that there was no hope for constitutional advances, and accepted the British proposal to increase in kind the non-Muslim and official (British) members of the

---

[17] Georghallides, *A Political and Administrative History*, 205–9, 230, 249–52, 288, 345; Varnava, *British Cyprus and the Long Great War*, 158–59, 165, 175, 177–78, 185–201, 205, 210.

[18] *Ελευθερία*, 3 December 1921, 1; *Ελευθερία*, 27 February 1929, 1; Georghallides, *A Political and Administrative History*, 210–11.

[19] The push for self-determination may have been decided upon the advice of Arthur Crosfield, see CO67/209/63025, confidential, Crosfield to FO, 20 December 1922; Georghallides, *A Political and Administrative History*, 208–9, 230–31; Varnava, *British Cyprus and the Long Great War*, 185–207.

legislative council, thus there was no change to the overall balance.[20] On the day before, Triantafyllides wrote to the British authorities on the economic situation, which was published on 8 September in *Ελευθερία*.[21] He argued that the post-war economic crisis was caused by a lack of confidence in the economy and not by a lack of revenue, referring to idle bank deposits. Distrust in the economy had developed after the 1919 anti-usury laws, as the middle class of lenders could no longer collect their debts, forcing their debtors into bankruptcy. Triantafyllides wanted the government to guarantee the loans, assume the mortgages and institute loan repayments at a rate of eight per cent. Also, he wanted an agricultural bank for the peasantry.[22] This public intervention showed his care for the Cypriot people beyond *enosis* and a willingness to work with the British to develop the island.

In May 1925 Cyprus became a Crown Colony. This was an emphatic indication that the British were staying, although the nationalists did not care and protested. Triantafyllides (see Figure 1.2)[23] called for the development of the country in order to pursue *enosis*. He was not the only one. Ioannis Clerides, Loizos Philippou, a lawyer and editor of the newspaper *Πάφος* (Paphos), and Stelios Pavlides (see Figure 1.2),[24] who was married to Theodotou's other daughter, thus the brother-in-law of Triantafyllides, all called for the end to the boycott of the legislative council, close cooperation with the British and Turkish Cypriots and for a campaign for a new constitution, because self-government did not negatively affect the chances of *enosis*.[25] In the 1925 elections for the legislative council, the 'national council' decided to field candidates. Triantafyllides withdrew his interest to facilitate cooperation, but no common ground was found. Instead three factions emerged: nationalists, whom Triantafyllides supported, namely Theodotou, Paschalis (see Figure 1.2),[26] Demosthenis Severis and George Markides, who demanded a new constitution as a prelude to *enosis*; 'populists' advocating closer cooperation with the British and Turkish Cypriots, and a reduced role for the church, to achieve agricultural reform, under George Hadji Pavlou, his brother Fedon Ioannides and Stavros G. Stavrinakis, all advocates; and 'moderates', advocating cooperation with the British and Turkish Cypriots to develop the island as a prelude to self-government, namely Panayiotis Cacoyannis, Stelios Pavlides,

---

[20] Varnava, *British Cyprus and the Long Great War*, 206–7.
[21] *Ελευθερία*, 8 September 1923, 1.
[22] Georghallides, *A Political and Administrative History of Cyprus*, 296.
[23] Triantafyllides is in the middle row, third from left.
[24] Pavlides is the tall gentleman in the top row, with a bow tie, second from right.
[25] Georghallides, *A Political and Administrative History of Cyprus*, 344–45, 411.
[26] Paschalis is the tall gentleman in the top row, wearing a wig, seventh from left.

Figure 1.2 Triantafyllides with other members of the Legal Fraternity, 1927.

Source: Courtesy of Agni Michaelidou, Χώρα, η Παληά Λευκωσία (Country, Old Nicosia), Nicosia, 1974.

Neophytos Nicolaides, all lawyers, and Hadji Eftychios Hadji Procopi, a landowner and agriculturalist. The elections were a disaster for the nationalists, as the moderates and populists won most of the seats.[27]

It was not until 1930 that Triantafyllides, now a leading lawyer, formally entered politics when he ran for the legislative council for the Morphou-Lefka constituency.[28] He confirmed his candidature on 4 October and was supported by Ελευθερία, Bishop Makarios and Dr Ioannis Pigasiou, as they agreed that the masses would come to support *enosis* with their economic amelioration.[29] Makarios had also quarrelled with Triantafyllides's opponent, the incumbent, Hadji Pavlou (who studied law in Athens at the same time as Triantafyllides and probably knew each other then), the 'populist' who had defeated Paschalis in 1925 and had attacked both the church and Paschalis and Pavlides for accepting the roles of Solicitor General and Crown counsel respectively in 1927.[30]

---

[27] Varnava, *British Cyprus and the Long Great War*, 203–11.
[28] Ελευθερία, 13 September 1930, 3.
[29] Irene Pophaides, 'Kyrillos III, 1916–33: Between Sophronios III and Kyrillos II', in Varnava and Michael (eds), *The Archbishops of Cyprus in the Modern Age*, 177–209, 203.
[30] Katsourides, *Greek Cypriot Nationalist Right*, 152–54.

In his manifesto, Triantafyllides declared that he was running as the 'nationalist-rural' candidate to fight for the development of Cyprus and for *enosis*. For him the prosperity of the rural population was pivotal, because agriculture was the heart of the economy, and when it prospered so too did other classes.[31] During the campaign, a colourful caricature depicted Hadji Pavlou, the 'populist', being chased by his people into the roses, whose thorns had ruined him (see Figure 1.3).[32] After the 1925 disaster, there was a minor nationalist comeback, helped by the withdrawal of Cacoyannis, Hadji Procopi, and Nicolaides (Pavlides resigned in 1927), who had endured personal attacks from Theodotou and Makarios. In any event, Triantafyllides beat Hadji Pavlou (15–16 October) by 134 votes.[33] On 22 October, *Ελευθερία* published a letter signed by 'K', which endorsed the election of Triantafyllides because he would be a 'true PanCypriot member' and unlike other leaders, was possessed with a cool pragmatism that would bring him and the island success.[34] Then on 28 October, within two weeks, he also accepted the British offer to join the executive council, replacing Cacoyannis.[35] This was interesting because, only the year before, the government had asked Stavros Stavrinakis to resign from the executive council because he had failed to support a measure in the legislative council that he had supported in the executive council, so the authorities believed that they could rely on Triantafyllides to not do the same thing.[36]

His acceptance of the British offer enraged his extremist, now former, supporters, who promptly attacked him in the newspapers. The editor of *Νέος Κυπριακός Φύλαξ* attacked Triantafyllides because he claimed that the executive council had shadowy powers and Triantafyllides would be restricted from expressing himself in the legislative council.[37] The most vicious attacks came from Savvas Loizides, a leader of a secret nationalist society formed in Kyrenia in 1929. Loizides, like Triantafyllides, had studied law in Athens, in his case during the turbulent years from 1920 to 1922, and his postgraduate studies in

---

[31] *Χρόνος* (Year), 4 October 1930, 3; *Ελευθερία*, 8 October 1930, 3. Georghallides, *Cyprus and the Governorship of Sir Ronald Storrs*, 212, 377–78.

[32] Roses referred to Triantafyllides's name, which means rosewood.

[33] *Ελευθερία*, 18 October 1930, 2. Varnava, *British Cyprus and the Long Great War*, 195, 201, 210; Georghallides, *Cyprus and the Governorship of Sir Ronald Storrs*, 380–81.

[34] *Ελευθερία*, 22 October 1930, 2. 'K' could have been anyone, including Ioannis Clerides, who also wrote for *Ελευθερία*.

[35] *Ελευθερία*, 1 November 1930, 2. See also, Georghallides, *Cyprus and the Governorship of Sir Ronald Storrs*, 380–81.

[36] CO67/227/1, confidential, Nicholson (acting governor) to Amery, 30 March 1929. Also, FCO141/2416.

[37] *Νέος Κυπριακός Φύλαξ* (New Cypriot Guardian), 5 November 1930, 4; *Νέος Κυπριακός Φύλαξ*, 19 November 1930, 4; *Νέος Κυπριακός Φύλαξ*, 3 December 1930, 1.

Figure: 1.3 (above) 'Ο ΛΑΙΚΟΣ ΚΑΤΑΔΙΩΚΟΜΕΝΟΣ ΥΠΟ ΤΟΥ ΛΑΟΥ ΤΟΥ (below) Αχ! αυτά τα αγκάθια τις τριανταφυλλιάς με κατέστρεψαν ((above) THE POPULIST CHASED BY THEIR PEOPLE (below) Ah! these rose thorns have ruined me). Cartoon from the 1930 elections for the legislative council, depicting Hadji Pavlou being chased into thorny rose bushes by peasants and labourers supporting Triantafyllides, *Κύπρος* (Cyprus), Limassol, 1930.

Source: Courtesy of Stelios A. Triantafyllides, Nicosia, Cyprus.

Heidelberg and Göttingen from 1922 to 25, during the early rise of Nazism. He then returned to Kyrenia and practised law and journalism.[38] He was the leading force, along with Bishop Makarios, in the secret nationalist society (mimicking the Friendly Society from the Greek War of Independence over 100 years earlier), which became EREK (National Radical Union of Cyprus), and as he boasted in his memoirs, 'Kyrenia was [then] the Acropolis of the *enosis* struggle'. He was notorious for his vitriol against anyone who wavered on *enosis*; referring to those working within the British colonial system as 'reformist', while 'infernals' were those accepting government posts. Aside from Hadji Pavlou, there had been rejoicing upon the appointments of Paschalis and Pavlides

---

[38] Loizides, *Άτυχη Κύπρος*, 14–20.

in 1927 because various memorials to the British authorities demanded that Cypriots be appointed to government positions.[39] Paschalis, Pavlides and now Triantafyllides received Loizides's stick when he joined the executive council because Triantafyllides had been elected to the legislative council with Loizides's support. His attack on Triantafyllides and others who agreed with him was bitter and personal, as he rejected the aim to improve the lives of Cypriots, as this would happen after *enosis*, which should be the only goal.[40]

Triantafyllides defended himself in three letters published in *Ελευθερία*. He referred to the numerous pro-*enosis* figures of previous generations, including Kyrillos, then Bishop of Kitium, later Archbishop Kyrillos II, Christodoulos Sozos, a martyr of the Balkan Wars, who had been called a traitor for suggesting that the Greek Cypriots campaign for independence as a prelude to *enosis*;[41] and even Theodotou, all of whom had been members of both councils and had combined their support for *enosis* with their work to contribute towards the development of the island. He also claimed that the governor, Sir Ronald Storrs, who succeeded Stevenson, had assured him that he could express any views in both councils without reservation. He believed that any of the other elected members, who had not opposed his acceptance, would have accepted his joining because there was no policy of rejecting such positions and anyone accepting them was serving the best interests of the country.[42] With Triantafyllides, *Ελευθερία* sat on the fence, but Georghallides believed that it disagreed with his decision. In any event, on 7 November Hadji Pavlou challenged the election, accusing Triantafyllides of offering bribes for votes. The court annulled the election in April 1931 and Triantafyllides did not contest the by-election.[43]

While a member of both councils, Triantafyllides showed that he was not afraid to criticise the British authorities. He criticised the government's planned spending for 1931, challenging its revenue projections, and arguing that it

---

[39] See FCO141/2403; Rappas, 'The Cypriot Colonial Civil Servant', 125–27. Storrs claimed that Paschalis had one of the best practices in the island at that time. CO27/220/4, confidential, Storrs to Amery, 25 January 1927.

[40] Loizides, *Άτυχη Κύπρος*, 21–29, 37, 73; Kypros Chrysanthis, 'Ιστορικά Δεδομένα σχετικά με το κίνημα του 1931' [Historical Facts on the Movement of 1931], *Πρακτικά του Πρώτου Διεθνούς Κυπριολογικού Συνεδρίου, Λευκοσία 14–19 Απριλίου 1969* [First International Congress of Cypriot Studies, Nicosia 14–19 April 1969], 3(a), Nicosia, 1973, 451–56; Georghallides, *Cyprus and the Governorship of Sir Ronald Storrs*, 408–10, 414–17, 600–2, 642–43, 685; Varnava, *British Imperialism in Cyprus*, 184; Alecou, *Communism and Nationalism in Postwar Cyprus*, 16.

[41] Varnava, *British Imperialism in Cyprus*, 262.

[42] *Ελευθερία*, 12 November 1930, 2; *Ελευθερία*, 15 November 1930, 2; *Ελευθερία*, 26 November 1930, 2. See also Georghallides, *Cyprus and the Governorship of Sir Ronald Storrs*, 406.

[43] *Ελευθερία*, 18 April 1931, 2.

had to reduce its projected expenditure from about £800,000 to £725,000. He deplored the suggestion to touch the reserve fund of £90,000 which he considered 'sacred' and only for an emergency. For him there was no emergency yet, but he was concerned about the Great Depression hitting Cyprus harder in 1931, so the cost to run the government and bureaucracy needed scaling back to balance the budget. This meant cutting the highest salaries, but not the minimum wage of civil servants. He also suggested restructuring the economy and reducing state expenditure; a reduction in the interest offered to peasant farmers by the Agricultural Bank; and the introduction of a social security scheme, a progressive idea then.[44] Triantafyllides considered social and economic development as paramount to achieving *enosis*, and would not rule out self-government as a prelude to *enosis*.[45]

Such a stance, however, incensed the extremists. As early as January 1931, while still a member of both councils, Triantafyllides continued to be criticised, as were Paschalis and Pavlides. On 3 January the pro-Royalist Athenian newspaper *Πρωϊα* (Morning) published an article by George Melopoulos, which was reproduced on 23 January in *Αλήθεια* (Truth) in Limassol. As Georghallides correctly observed, the article resembled the rhetoric of Savvas Loizides. Melopoulos claimed to be a Greek merchant who had just returned to Athens after spending four months in Cyprus. He argued that Cypriot politicians were divided into those who were true patriots, Greek nationalists who genuinely desired *enosis*, represented the views of the rural population (a rhetorical theme of the far right) and were disinterested in serving British imperial interests; and 'moderates' who only paid lip service to *enosis*, and were really working for their own career advancement and for the British imperial aim of creating 'a narrow Cypriot nationalism'. He told his Greek readers that there was a pro-British party now in Cyprus under Paschalis and Pavlides, who had changed overnight from passionate nationalists to 'traitors'. Then there were the actions of others, such as Triantafyllides, who joined the executive council to be the willing tools of the British imperialists. Melopoulos also referred to the elections to the legislative council as corrupted by the payment of bribes to electors and the provision of food and drink to people to vote. This was in reference to the accusations against Triantafyllides, although it was

---

[44] *Minutes of the Legislative Council of Cyprus for 1929*, Nicosia, 1930; *Φωνή της Κύπρου*, 29 November 1930, 3; *Νέος Κυπριακός Φύλαξ*, 3 December 1930, 3. For a discussion on this, see, Georghallides, *Cyprus and the Governorship of Sir Ronald Storrs*, 438–40. Peter Clarke and Andrekos Varnava, 'Accounting in Cyprus during British Rule, Post-World War I to Independence', *Accounting History* 18, no. 3 (2013): 293–315.

[45] He also proposed other initiatives, see *Φωνή της Κύπρου*, 27 December 1930, 2; *Ελευθερία*, 28 January 1931, 2.

acknowledged that Triantafyllides had merely funded the travel of supporters to vote, as many others had done in the past and present (Theodotou had successfully fought off a similar charge in court).[46]

As for Melopoulos, he was soon accused of being a fake in a letter in *Ελευθερία* by an anonymous author, which Georghallides seemed to agree with. The author claimed that there was no such person as George Melopoulos visiting Cyprus and that a Cypriot created him to hide behind a fake Greek identity to offer legitimacy to the attack on individuals. The author countered Melopoulos's critique without emotion or personal animosity. Much of the evidence and reasoning had been given before by Triantafyllides, namely that there was no boycott of cooperating with the government while the country was being developed in order to prepare the ground for a movement for *enosis* and many in earlier generations had done so. The criticism against Triantafyllides for joining the executive council was unfounded, since never before had anyone rejected such an offer, and it was unclear why Triantafyllides should have. Previous memorials (including that delivered by a deputation in 1929) to London had asked that Cypriots be appointed to all positions in the government with the exceptions of colonial secretary, treasurer and attorney general, and the fact that the British authorities were starting to fill certain positions with locals reflected the success of the policy. Therefore, 'Melopoulos' was being mischievous and toed the line peddled by a tiny minority of extremists in Cyprus who opposed the accepted policy. The writing, particularly the meticulous composition of the argument, resembled the writing of Triantafyllides.[47]

In any event, Triantafyllides stepped back. He did not contest the by-election on 9 May, but his withdrawal from politics was temporary. He claimed that there could be constitutional changes soon and did not want to recontest under a system which damned him for using the same methods as others. He was, of course, criticised for not running to avoid being 'punished' by the electors for joining the executive council.[48] But he also had his supporters. The

---

[46] *Νέος Κυπριακός Φύλαξ*, 22 April 1931, 3; Georghallides, *Cyprus and the Governorship of Sir Ronald Storrs*, 518–21, 568. There was a second letter (signed Nicolaos Skoufas, the name of one of the founders of the Friendly Society in 1814) published in the Greek newspapers, claiming that Paschalis and Pavlides were going to resign after reading Melopoulos's article. This time a Cypriot signing himself as 'Lefkosiatis' (a person of Nicosia) criticised the article as ridiculous, especially for claiming that the only patriots were those who were extremist and confrontational. Ibid., 520–22.

[47] Ibid., 598–600. It could also have been Ioannis Clerides.

[48] *Νέος Κυπριακός Φύλαξ*, 13 May 1931, 3. For further discussion see, Georghallides, *Cyprus and the Governorship of Sir Ronald Storrs*, 644. Triantfyllides's comment about changes may have referred to the decision by Storrs to open up senior positions in the government to Cypriots. See FCO141/2454.

editor of *Πάφος* (Philippou) stated that no other member of the legislative council had opposed Triantafyllides joining the executive council and that he had temporarily withdrawn from politics for it would be an injustice if he had withdrawn permanently, because he was the best politician.[49]

By now Triantafyllides openly supported Venizelos's political stance, who was again prime minister (1928–32). Venizelos, as he had told Triantafyllides back in 1920, continued to believe in following the constitutional path, as he also told the disruptive Alexis Kyrou, his volatile Greek consul in Cyprus, in May 1931, because the policy of confrontation would fail.[50] Triantafyllides had lost the support of the fanatical nationalists, something that he clearly did not mind given their divergent paths, and looked on with concern at the rise of EREK, led largely by Loizides (Stylianou claimed that Loizides was the leader) and Makarios, which opposed cooperation with the British and self-government, and demanded only *enosis*.[51] The founding members of EREK took a 10-point oath on 18 October 1931, which included their aim for 'the fanatical pursuit of the union of Cyprus with the Greek political whole' and their opposition to 'any co-operation with the foreign Government in its legislative, executive, or administrative jurisdiction'.[52] They added that

> They shall regard as an enemy of their country any Greek inhabitant of the Island whose conduct is opposed to or in any way slackens the national struggle, which has one aim – union and nothing but union.[53]

Amongst the signatories were the leading far right pro-*enosis* extremists who seemingly plotted the assassination of Triantafyllides, namely, Evagoras Papa Nicolaou, Theophanis Tsangarides, Dr Pigasiou (who no longer cared about the economic development of the rural population), Polycarpos S. Ioannides (who was raised by Bishop Makarios),[54] and Loizides. Makarios was not a signatory, but the force and finance behind EREK. This group played a pivotal role in the collision with the British over *enosis* in October 1931: first, by placing pressure on moderates and particularly the Bishop of

---

[49] *Πάφος*, 19 June 1931, 3.
[50] Stylianou, *Το Κίνημα του Οκτώβρη του 1931 στην Κύπρο*, 248.
[51] Ibid., 57. For a further discussion of EREK and Loizides's extremist views see Georghallides, *Cyprus and the Governorship of Sir Ronald Storrs*, 414–18, 600–2; Katsourides, *Greek Cypriot Nationalist Right*, 159–62.
[52] Stylianou, *Το Κίνημα του Οκτώβρη του 1931 στην Κύπρο*, 57–58; Jan Asmussen, 'Disturbances in Cyprus in October, 1931', *Journal of Cyprus Studies* 12 (2006): 5–55, Appendix 5, EREK Oath, 18 October 1931, 45–48.
[53] Ibid.
[54] See FCO141/4281, top secret, KEK Dossier, 1949.

Kitium, Nicodemos, to take a stronger position; second, through the actions of some on 21 October and in the immediate aftermath in spreading the riots to Kyrenia; and third, by inspiring other extremists, such as in Famagusta, where a declaration was issued that included a demand, and the use of violence if necessary, to force Paschalis and Pavlides to resign from their government posts.[55] Loizides, Tsangarides, Kolokasides and Makarios were deported for their roles in the riots. Tsangarides was characterised as one of the 'most violent members of EREK', while Kolokasides was known to write vitriolic anti-government articles in the Athenian press.[56] Triantafyllides's part in the October events was minimal, as he watched his predictions of a messy clash unfold.

The causes of the 1931 riots are debated between three schools of thought. The 'nationalist school' claims that the riots were a Greek Cypriot national awakening against alien British rule in favour of *enosis*, or put differently, a manifestation of anti-colonialism expressed as *enosis*.[57] Then there is the 'socio-economic school', which refers to the local attacks (involving the Cypriot peasant and labouring classes from all religious/ethnic backgrounds) on agricultural production, processing and storage, driven by the long-term limited agricultural development and the Great Depression, and that any nationalism was the opportunism of the tiny group of divided Greek Cypriot political elites who haphazardly attempted to capitalise by leading a 'national revolt'.[58] Third, those who argue for a 'combination', but who gave too much validity to the nationalists by understanding economic

---

[55] Stylianou, *Το Κίνημα του Οκτώβρη του 1931 στην Κύπρο*, 57–58, 91–3, 111–21; Katsiaounis, 'Cyprus 1931–1959', 446; Ioannides, *Cyprus under British Colonial Rule*, 173–78.

[56] Georghallides, 'The Cyprus Revolt', 77–78.

[57] Georghallides, *Cyprus and the Governorship of Sir Ronald Storrs*; Georghallides, 'The Cyprus Revolt'; Georghallides, 'Church and State in Cyprus'; Georghallides, 'British Policy on Cyprus During 1931'; Holland, *Britain and the Revolt in Cyprus*, 1–19; Stylianou, *Το Κίνημα του Οκτώβρη του 1931 στην Κύπρο*; Holland and Markides, *The British and the Hellenes*, 162–88; Ioannides, *Cyprus under British Colonial Rule*, 170–83.

[58] Reginald Nicholson, 'The Riots in Cyprus', *The Nineteenth Century* 110 Dec. (1931): 685–93; Major-General Sir Charles W. Gwynn, *Imperial Policing* (London 1936), 331–66. Rappas, *Cyprus in the 1930s*, 11. I agree with this thesis. Vatiliotis, one of the CPC leaders, in his report in February 1932 on the events of October 1931 also argued that they were primarily driven by economic and social conditions. Manolis Choumerianos and Spyros Sakellaropoulos, 'The Communist Party of Cyprus, the Comintern and the Uprising of 1931: Thoughts on the "apologia" of Charalambos Vatyliotis (Vatis)', *Twentieth Century Communism* 16 (2019): 103–124, 109–110. Additionally, there are similarities with the Scottish food riots of the previous century. See Eric Richards, *The Last Scottish Food Riots*, No. 6, *Past & Present*, 1982.

hardship and anti-government activities as anti-colonialism and pro-*enosis* nationalism.[59]

By October 1931 four political forces had emerged in Cyprus. The communists, who had grown steadily, appealed to workers, sought cooperation with Turkish Cypriots, and opposed *enosis* in favour of self-government that would lead to independence as a Cypriot Republic in a socialist Balkan federation. They stayed largely out of the events of 1931, initially denouncing it as 'chauvinistic' and 'bourgeoisie', until late when their leaders, particularly Haralambos Vatiliotis (Vatis), accepted that this was an opportunity to unite with the nationalist Right in an 'anti-imperial revolt'.[60] Regardless, the Nicosia Section of the CPC warned in May 1932 that *enosis* was a false paradise, Greece was bankrupt and 'our mother-land (USSR) is preparing the table on which we shall devour Imperialism'.[61] Then there were several nationalist right-wing groups. One, largely behind Bishop Nicodemos of Kitium (second group), had first supported a mass campaign of civil disobedience, only to pull back at the eleventh hour. This angered some within this group, including Theodotou, and infuriated Loizides and Makarios, who announced EREK (third group) and their uncompromising views on *enosis* by any means. Finally, a fourth group that was still trying to work within legal means: the broader church of politicians behind Archbishop Kyrillos continued to support the 1929 memorial and for Cypriots to accept government positions to affect change from within. Triantafyllides belonged to this group. As late as 10 October, in a marathon meeting chaired by Kyrillos, Triantafyllides accepted the nomination to fill a gap in Nicosia's 'national council' after extremists resigned. His aim was to prevent an escalation, which initially worked as the meeting decided to abandon civil disobedience, but failed as more hardliners pushed the crisis to boiling point, and those previously less inclined to challenge the British at that moment.[62]

Triantafyllides's warning of a violent clash with the British and his abhorrence at the events that saw Government House (including the vast and precious collection of antiquities owned by Storrs) become ashes, were well known, even to Storrs. In his unpublished memoirs, Charles Belcher, the Australian lawyer and parliamentarian, and British colonial jurist, the Chief Justice of Cyprus from 1927 to 30, commented that Triantafyllides 'was very

---

[59] Hill, *A History of Cyprus*, 480–82, 546–50; Choumerianos and Sakellaropoulos, 'The Communist Party of Cyprus', 103–24.
[60] Katsourides, *The History of the Communist Party in Cyprus*, 139–40, 174–77.
[61] Sir Ronald Storrs Papers, Pembroke College, Cambridge, University of Melbourne microfilm collection (hereafter Storrs Papers), Box IV/2, Decision of the Central Committee of the CPC and Local Committee, Nicosia Section, 24 May 1932.
[62] Georghallides, *Cyprus and the Governorship of Sir Ronald Storrs*, 599, 685–87.

able, a bit of a humourist, and the only person I could find in Nicosia who could give Storrs a run at chess', indicating that Triantafyllides and Storrs occasionally passed the time together socially.[63] Although Storrs did not mention Triantafyllides in his memoirs, he did feel

> consolation in the absolute loyalty of the Cypriot Civil Servants, from the highest to the lowest; manifested no less in the brilliant advice of Neoptolemos Paschalis, the Cypriot Solicitor-General, than in the steadfast courage of the scores of constables, Greek as well as Turk, risking their lives day and night against mobs of exultant hooligans.[64]

As regards Triantafyllides, Charles Hart-Davis, the district commissioner of Nicosia, told Storrs on 28 October that:

> Mr A. Triantafyllides has asked me to convey to his excellency his deep personal regret for what happened on Wednesday night (when Government House was burned down) and his personal sympathy in the great loss which that destruction has brought on Sir Ronald (i.e. his antiquities collection).
>
> He added that he thought it was a very great mistake that the Archbishop did not do this when he had the opportunity at an interview.[65]

Then on 6 November, Evagoras G. Savvides, an advocate from Famagusta, sympathised to Storrs over 'the criminal acts' against Government House, assuring him that 'all the law-abiding citizens heard with indignation the deplorable attitude of the Nicosia mob'. He was

> one of the few Cypriots who before these events could see where the agitators were driving the country.
>
> Now the great majority of the people can see that, and may realise that the sound policy followed by honest politicians like Mr Triantafyllides whom the agitators declared and still consider a traitor was the only sincere policy for the welfare of the country.[66]

---

[63] MSS Brit Emp s347, unpublished memoirs of Charles Frederic Belcher, Bodleian Library, Special Collections, University of Oxford. Belcher was born in Geelong, Victoria, Australia.
[64] Sir Ronald Storrs, *Orientations* (London: Readers Union, 1939), 582.
[65] Storrs Papers, Box IV/3, Hart-Davis to Gunnis, 28 October 1931. The loss referred to Storrs's antiquities.
[66] Ibid., Evagoras G. Savvides, Varosha, to Storrs, 6 November 1931.

Savvides, as a lawyer, must have known Triantafyllides and his views well, and of the attacks on Triantafyllides from the pro-*enosis* far right, which Savvides opposed and deplored.

These two sources, albeit secondary, reflect Triantafyllides's alienation from the fanatical nationalists before the events of 21 October and his growing reputation for believing that *enosis* could be achieved only by cooperating with the British to develop the island, which was the position of Venizelos.[67] Yet when Makarios was in central prison before his deportation, he asked Storrs to see his lawyer, who was none other than Triantafyllides.[68] Regardless of whether the extremists considered him 'a traitor', they still considered Triantafyllides the best lawyer in the country. He represented many in court over the events of October 1931.[69] One of them, the 'socialist' former member of the legislative council, Christodoulos Galatopoulos, was unhappy about this, but accepted Triantafyllides because his wife, the sister of Panayiotis Cacoyiannis, wanted him.[70] Then later in 1932 Triantafyllides represented Leontios, the Bishop of Paphos, in his trial for sedition, in which Triantafyllides, Ioannis Clerides and Archbishop Kyrillos III, convinced Leontios to plead guilty and sign a declaration (prepared by Triantafyllides and Henry Blackall, the Attorney General) to not participate in seditious politics again, in exchange for not going to prison.[71] Leontios seemingly regretted this deal, spoke negatively of his lawyers, possibly blaming Triantafyllides, which may explain why at his funeral he did not deliver a eulogy or accompany the coffin to the cemetery, resulting in public comment.[72]

After the British revoked the constitution in 1931, there were discussions on introducing another, along the standard practices in other colonies,

---

[67] Pikros, *Ο Βενιζέλος και το Κυπριακό*, 67–114; Georghallides, *Cyprus and the Governorship of Sir Ronald Storrs*, 535–40.
[68] FCO141/2453, L. Gee, to Inspector of Prisons, 27 October 1931, enclosing, Makarios to Gee, undated.
[69] *Ελευθερία*, 30 April 1932, 4; *Νέος Κυπριακός Φύλαξ*, 22 June 1932, 2.
[70] Christodoulos Aristotle Galatopoulos, *From the Cruiser to the Jail Birds' Nest*, ed. and intro., Petros Stylianou (Nicosia: Museum Struggle, 1980), 108, 128–32. For reports of his arrest see *Evening Telegraph*, 27 October 1931, 5.
[71] See FCO141/2448, FCO141/2449, and CO67/243/4, Henniker-Heaton to Cunliffe-Lister, 18 November 1932, enclosing Blackall's report, 18 November 1932. See also, Harry Stamelos, 'A Case Study of State and Law in the Interwar Period: The Three Historic Criminal Trials of Bishop of Paphos Leontios during the British Rule in Cyprus (1932, 1938, 1939)', *Athens Journal of Law* 6, no. 1 (2020): 75–102, 92–93.
[72] CO67/243/4, report by M. Kareklas, LCCP, Paphos, 22 November 1932; FCO141/2464, secret, Hart-Davis to Colonial Secretary, 14 April 1934.

especially Malta.⁷³ One proposal from Paschalis in May 1932 was for a nominated council, for which he distributed a shortlist of possible members, which included Triantafyllides, and a who's who of centre-right figures, Nicholas G. Chrysafinis, Themistocles Dervis, Kyrillos K. Pavlides, Demetrios N. Demetriou, George Aradippiotis, George Vassiliades, Michael Valdaserides, Neophytos Nicolaides, Panayiotis Cacoyannis, Demosthenis Severis, Loizos Philippou and Nicholas P. Lanitis.⁷⁴ In the summer of 1933, Sir Reginald Stubbs (see Figure 1.4), who had replaced Storrs in October 1932, proposed exactly this, a nominated advisory council of four Christians and one Muslim, which Philip Cunliffe-Lister, the Secretary of State for the Colonies, supported. Cunliffe-Lister told Stubbs on 3 August 1933 that it was vital in making selections to keep in mind the importance of 'associating some of the best men in the island with Government'.⁷⁵ On 16 August Stubbs informed Cunliffe-Lister that because the Athenian press had been attacking the Cypriot government (Loizides, Kolokasides, Tsangarides and Makarios were in Athens and propagandising in favour of *enosis*) he did not want to announce that the advisory council was a prelude to a new constitution.⁷⁶ Stubbs was also concerned because Archbishop Kyrillos, whom he called 'that old ass',⁷⁷ was establishing a 'non-Cooperation movement [in which] the leading men were to refuse to assist the Government by serving on Boards or Committees and so forth', thus adopting the methods advocated by the extremists.⁷⁸ Consequently, he added again the reliable advocate from Limassol, Panayiotis Cacoyannis,⁷⁹ to the executive council, which would sit with the advisory council, but had not decided on the composition of the latter, except, as he told Cunliffe-Lister:

> I think that Triantafyllides, whom you met and disliked, will do. He is the son-in-law of a deportee but I don't think that will affect

---

[73] Iliya Marovich-Old, 'Nationalism as Resistance to Colonialism: A Comparative Look at Malta and Cyprus from 1919 to 1940', in *Cypriot Nationalisms in Context*, ed. Thekla Kyritsi and Nikos Christofis (Cham: Palgrave Macmillan, 2018), 261–81.
[74] See FCO141/2422.
[75] CO67/251/16, Cunliffe-Lister to Stubbs, 3 August 1933.
[76] CO67/251/7, private & personal, Stubbs to Cunliffe-Lister, 16 August 1933.
[77] CO67/251/16, Stubbs to Cunliffe-Lister, 26 August 1933.
[78] CO67/251/7, private & personal, Stubbs to Cunliffe-Lister, 16 August 1933.
[79] Panayiotis Loizos Cacoyannis (sometimes Kakoyannis) had been a member of the legislative council, 1925–30 and the executive council, 1929–31, and again from 1933 to 46, was knighted in 1936, and was the father of Michael Cacoyannis, the director of *Zorba the Greek* (1964).

Figure 1.4 Sir Reginald Edward Stubbs, c. 1925.

Source: Government Public Record Office, Hong Kong. Photo in the public domain according to Section 17 in Chapter 528 (Copyright Ordinance) of the Law of Hong Kong.

him. He is clever and I doubt if he is more dishonest than most people.[80]

Blackall, the Attorney General, had recommended Triantafyllides,[81] and he was the first choice for Stubbs because he was intelligent and would speak freely (despite being Theodotou's son-in-law). Cunliffe-Lister replied: 'I shall not object to Triantafyllides: a rose, etc....'.[82] By now, Triantafyllides earned £5,000 a year according to Theodotou, much more than the Governor.[83]

---

[80] CO67/251/7, private & personal, Stubbs to Cunliffe-Lister, 16 August 1933.
[81] MSS Brit Emp s447, Blackall Papers, Blackall notes beneath translated article from Πατρίς.
[82] CO67/251/7, private & personal, Cunliffe-Lister to Stubbs, 24 August 1933. Rose referred to his name, which means rosewood in Greek. Cunliffe-Lister discussed his visit to Cyprus in his memoirs, but does not mention meeting Triantafyllides. Swinton, *I Remember*, 85–88.
[83] FCO141/2497, strictly confidential, Theodotou to Cunliffe-Lister, 26 January 1934; *Cyprus Blue Book for 1935*, CGPO, Nicosia, 1936, 151.

On 11 October Stubbs invited the four Greek Cypriots, Triantafyllides, Neophytos Nicolaides, a merchant and large landowner of Paphos and a former member of the legislative council (1925–30), Michalakis J. Louisides, a merchant, orange grower and the deputy mayor of Famagusta, and Paul George Pavlides, a merchant and landowner of Limassol (first cousin of Stelios Pavlides), to join an advisory council to 'enable the Government to keep itself informed of the views and feelings of the Community to a greater extent than is possible in present circumstances'. Along with the members of the executive council, they would discuss laws, the annual estimates, public health, education and infrastructure, and could freely raise and express themselves, but decisions rested with the governor.[84] Triantafyllides was the first to accept:

> I accept with pleasure the honour bestowed upon me in the earnest hope that the creation of such a council will under the circumstances tend to improve the present conditions of the colony. I may say, your Excellency, that I am fully alive to the difficulties of the situation and the responsibilities attached to my acceptance. But I consider it as my duty, as well as the duty of every good Cypriot, to respond [to] any call of the government and offer my humble contribution in the effort to ensure better days to the country.[85]

The three others invited also accepted,[86] but only Triantafyllides hinted at being 'alive to the difficulties', probably the opposition of the extremists. Stubbs, who was about to cut short his tenure in Cyprus to take up the governorship of Ceylon,[87] understood and was 'anxious' to 'discourage intrigue'

---

[84] FCO141/2493, confidential, Stubbs to Nicolaides, Louizides, Pavlides and Triantafyllides, 11 October 1933. Louisides, sometimes Louizides and Loizides, had no relation to Savvas Loizides.
[85] FCO141/2493, Triantafyllides to Stubbs, 12 October 1933.
[86] FCO141/2493, Pavlides to Stubbs, 13 October 1933; FCO141/2493, Lousides to Stubbs, 15 October 1933; FCO141/2493, confidentially, Nicolaides to Stubbs, 16 October 1933. As regards the Turkish Cypriot, Stubbs first invited Dr Raouf Potamializade, of Nicosia, who had never partaken in public service, but was 'a prominent and highly respected member of the community'. He did not accept because his English was weak and his practice was too busy. FCO141/2493, Stubbs to Cunliffe-Lister, 18 October 1933; FCO141/2493, Stubbs to Potamializade, 30 October 1933; Potamializade to Stubbs, 1 November 1933. Stubbs then invited Mehmed Zekia, an advocate from Famagusta, a Kemalist who had served in the last legislative council, who accepted. FCO141/2493, Stubbs to Zekia, 2 November 1933; Zekia to Stubbs, 6 November 1933.
[87] FCO141/2493, Stubbs to Cunliffe-Lister, 18 October 1933.

because he believed that the advisory council was 'the first step to a better state of affairs' and it would fail if *enosis* remained 'a real factor in public life'.[88] Indeed the announcement of its composition provoked 'unfavourable criticism, chiefly of a personal nature' against those who agreed to accept the British offers to join it.[89] Triantafyllides took the most stick because unlike the others he had been a prominent pro-*enosis* nationalist.

The attack was led by *Πρωτεύουσα* (Capital), the organ of Bishop Makarios, now in Athens after his deportation to London in 1931, and the remnants of EREK in Cyprus. Signed by P. Stylianou, the British believed it was by Polycarpos Stylianou Ioannides, a staffer of the newspaper and the secretary of the Kyrenia Diocese. The article on 1 November 1933 was a long vitriolic diatribe against the government and those who joined the advisory council, especially Triantafyllides.[90] The attack continued two days later in an editorial, which was even more aggressive and personal against the four Greek Cypriots who joined it.[91] As these attacks continued, the British authorities reimposed censorship on *Πρωτεύουσα*, no doubt angering Papa Nicolaou, Ioannides and Makarios.[92]

Triantafyllides had already publicly defended his decision. On 30 October he issued a statement, published in *Νέος Κυπριακός Φύλαξ* on 1 November, that the advisory council was a temporary measure to provide an interim period of stability before a new constitution could be introduced, and necessary because the Cypriots could hardly expect the reintroduction of a representative government or a better system than before because that would be seen as rewarding the violence of October 1931. He considered it his duty to help rebuild a climate of cooperation and trust with the British authorities, which was necessary before a new constitution, with representative government, could be reintroduced. It was also his duty to contribute to improving the lives of Cypriots and the advisory council could do that since it would examine the economic and social issues facing Cyprus.[93] Triantafyllides

---

[88] FCO141/2493, Stubbs to Shuckburgh, 3 November 1933.
[89] FCO141/2464, quarterly reports from police and district commissioners, October to December 1933, Palmer to Cunliffe-Lister, 19 January 1934.
[90] CO67/253/10, secret, Palmer to Cunliffe-Lister, 19 January 1934, including article, *Πρωτεύουσα* (Capital), 1 November 1933.
[91] CO67/253/10, secret, Palmer to Cunliffe-Lister, 19 January 1934, including article, *Πρωτεύουσα*, 3 November 1933.
[92] CO67/253/10, secret, Palmer to Cunliffe-Lister, 19 January 1934, enclosure, dossier on Evagoras Papa Nicolaou; See also FCO141/2496, when the suppression order was renewed.
[93] *Νέος Κυπριακός Φύλαξ*, 1 November 1933, 3.

responded to the criticism on 8 November in *Ελευθερία*, which included his response to a question by Odysseus Wideson, a former member of the legislative council (1922–24) and the correspondent for *Ελευθερία* in Larnaca.[94] Triantafyllides stated that he had read the criticisms of the advisory council and of his decision to accept, and would accept if his decision turned out wrong. But the criticisms against the formation of the advisory council missed the essence of the question. It was not representative, but it was a step forward to restore relations between the British authorities and Cypriots, improve political conditions and promote the development and interests of the island. He believed that after the violent events of 1931, which he called 'sad'.[95]

> it would be politically pointless and utterly naive to ask the Government to give us something better than the constitution which was abolished under the unanimous disapproval of the people.[96]

Our response, he argued, should be 'dignified', 'wise', and a 'sincere manifestation of cooperation […] to produce the reasonable hope for more political rights for Cypriots'. Triantafyllides took his politics seriously, evidenced from the epigram, to which he added: 'we should not confuse popular aspirations with the political means of achieving this end'. Wideson asked him how he could interpret the thoughts of the people since he was unelected, and he replied that as an educated Cypriot in public life, it was his responsibility to try and lead the people to achieve their aspirations, using any methods he judged as best to succeed.[97] On the same day, in an interview to *Πρωινή* (Morning), he added that it was after long reflection that he decided to cooperate with the British to develop the island before the Cypriot people could participate in a movement for national liberation. There were various methods to prosecute such a movement, violence was tried in October 1931 and it had led to the current anomalous situation, now it was time to try

---

[94] Wideson is another forgotten yet significant figure in Cypriot history (1920s to 1950s) as a journalist, politician, travel agent, Cyprus airways employee, and merchant in Larnaca. Like Triantafyllides he was also assassinated, in his case by EOKA in April 1956. In the Commons a statement from EOKA was read justifying the assassination as the 'necessary price for purification'. HoC, Sir Douglas Dodds-Parker, 2 July 1956, 84. Also, Crawshaw, *The Cyprus Revolt*, 175; Tabitha Morgan, *Sweet and Bitter Island: A History of the British in Cyprus* (London: I. B. Tauris, 2010), 193–94.

[95] *Ελευθερία*, 8 November 1933, 2.

[96] Ibid.

[97] Ibid.

cooperation, to bring about more rights and a new constitution to advance political culture.[98]

Demosthenis Stavrinides, the editor of *Ελευθερία*, his former supporter, did not sit on the fence, but was more guarded. In front-page editorials on 11 and 15 November, he stated that he wanted to believe Triantafyllides was right, but was sceptical of the process and the British motives. It was fine for Triantafyllides to claim that the advisory council was interim and that it was necessary, but the British had not stated this and he had not stated how long the interim period should last. There was no political philosophy or plan from the four Greek Cypriots joining the advisory council, and although Stavrinides respected Triantafyllides for his intelligence and national profile, he could not say the same for the other three. Ultimately, he was sceptical of the advisory council rebuilding relations between the government and the people.[99]

Before his departure, Stubbs told Cunliffe-Lister that the success of the advisory council was vital before introducing a new constitution, perhaps in two years. He criticised the Cypriot political establishment: 'I know of no community which is so utterly unfit to take any responsible part in the Government of the native country as is that of Cyprus [...] [and] public spirit is a thing not only unknown but practically inconceivable'. He claimed that in the other colonies where he had served (Hong Kong and Jamaica) many locals served the public good, but in Cyprus men only entered public life to profit themselves and their extended family and friends.[100] Constitutional advance, he argued, must be 'preceded by a considerable period of training in western civilisation', because the people 'still remain an Asiatic race', who had been unable to use their previous constitution.[101] These were strange observations because most of the Empire did not belong to western civilisation, yet he claimed that it participated in government, while Greek Cypriots would not – an orientalist othering *par excellence*. In any event, Stubbs believed that politically the two main threats were from communism and the church. He argued that the new Penal Laws would 'suppress the Communists altogether', and blamed the courts and judges for not siding with the government against them.[102]

---

[98] *Πρωινή*, 8 November 1933, 1.
[99] *Ελευθερία*, 11 November 1933, 1; *Ελευθερία*, 15 November 1933, 1. Similar criticisms were in *Νέος Κυπριακός Φύλαξ*, 15 November 1933, 1.
[100] CO67/251/3, Stubbs memorandum, 16 October 1933.
[101] Ibid.
[102] See FCO141/2455 for the penal laws against communism. This file has many retained pages.

As for the church, it was 'more difficult to deal with' and was baffled by its power when few people attended liturgy except for a few important days. Thus, he believed that the advisory council was a gamble worth taking.[103]

The advisory council met for the first time on 16 November 1933. It was the only meeting that Triantafyllides attended before being shot on 12 January 1934.[104]

---

[103] CO67/251/3, Stubbs memorandum, 16 October 1933.
[104] FCO141/2477, advisory council minutes, 16 November 1933. Present: Stubbs; Henniker-Heaton; H. W. B. Blackall, Attorney General; H. J. Pink, Treasurer; C. H. Hart-Davis, DCNic; P. L. Cacoyannis (EC); M. Munir Bey, OBE (EC); M. J. Louisides (AC); N. Nicolaides (AC); P. Pavlides (AC); A. Triantafyllides (AC); Zekia Bey (AC). The meeting dealt with estimates of expenditure for 1934, i.e. printing office, judiciary, police, prisons, health, education, forests, public works, levy on salaries. It was also the only meeting for Stubbs.

Chapter 2

THE COLONIAL NEWSPAPER ARCHIVE AND THE TRIANTAFYLLIDES CASE

Even if this long-suffering Island has known many wounds, not less than three months have passed and two wounds have been opened in its bowels.

Πρωινή (Morning), 18 January 1934, 1.

During the night of 12 January, many of the newspaper editors in Nicosia were in deep shock as news of the shooting of Antonios Triantafyllides spread. The editor of *Πρωινή* was at the hospital, where Dr Themistocles Dervis, the Mayor of Nicosia (1929–46 and 1949–59), stated that 'his situation was critical'.[1] As the editors went to press, they could only report on his shooting, and had no idea that their next print would be reporting his death, which caused much heartache and loss for his family, friends, colleagues and the public, as evidenced by the numerous published memorials, for example the epigram, which places the assassination of Triantafyllides on the same level of importance as that of Kyrillos III.[2]

This chapter explores the colonial newspapers which cover two periods of the Triantafyllides case. The first with articles on the shooting, his death and the funeral and memorial services. These provide the reactions (generally of shock and sadness) from the newspaper editors, the public and his friends and colleagues. The articles also establish a timeline of the before and after the shooting, until his death, with numerous important facts revealed that were not covered in the subsequent trial. These articles are vital for analysing the second series of articles, on the pre-hearing and criminal court case against Stavros Christodoulou, which took place a year after the assassination. Without

---

[1] *Πρωινή*, 13 January 1934, 4.
[2] *Πρωινή*, 18 January 1934, 1; *Χρόνος*, 22 January 1934, 1, in which it was stated that Triantafyllides had considered 13 his unlucky number, and interestingly so did Makarios III. See also poem by Akis Voreadis, *Φωνή της Κύπρου*, 20 January 1934, 4.

the court records or a comprehensive account of the court proceedings in the government files, the newspapers proved essential for establishing many facts in connection with the shooting, death, funeral and memorials, and the subsequent court case, especially the case of the prosecution and the testimonies of witnesses.

The chapter has two broad aims. Methodologically it aims to show that a community of records can only be created when all the sources are consulted, and in this case the newspapers proved pivotal to exploring the case because they provided information and detail otherwise unavailable. And second, the newspapers reveal the inner workings of Cypriot society, particularly in relation to the death and the various reactions to it, and of the subsequent trial as it played out in all its detail and unusual contradictions, particularly with the evidence of prosecution witnesses not supporting the case of the prosecution.

By the 1930s there were numerous Greek Cypriot newspapers which served the interests of owners and editors. The two most national newspapers were from Nicosia, *Ελευθερία*, edited by Demosthenis Stavrinides, which had been pro-Venizelist and Liberal, but which became more critical of Venizelos's Cyprus policy by the 1930s, and the more conservative and Greek-Royalist, *Φωνή της Κύπρου*. There was also the centrist *Πρωινή* which involved Kyriakos Kakoullis and Costas Ashiotis, later a senior civil servant during the British and Republican periods, and High Commissioner to London (1966–79). More anti-government and pro-*enosis* were *Νέος Κυπριακός Φύλαξ* and especially *Πρωτεύουσα*. In Limassol there were the nationalistic *Αλήθεια*, the moderate *Χρόνος* and *Παρατηρητής*, edited by Demetris Demetriades and the socialist Panos Fasouliotis (who were cousins) respectively, which supported working with the government to improve the island, as did *Πάφος*.[3]

The Shooting, Death and Reactions

When the initial articles went to press during the early hours of 13 January, informing the public of the shooting, Triantafyllides was still alive, perhaps that was why they were not on the front page. *Ελευθερία*, *Φωνή της Κύπρου* and *Πρωινή* reported on the shooting.[4] The details were mostly based on what Triantafyllides and the other eyewitness, especially Nicholas S. Coureas, his brother-in-law and neighbour, could relate. Triantafyllides had walked

---

[3] Coudounaris, *Βιογραφικόν Λεξικόν Κυπρίων*, 34, 68–69, 126, 383; Katsiaounis, *Η Διασκεπτική*, 21–22.

[4] *Ελευθερία*, 13 January 1934, 3; *Φωνή της Κύπρου*, 13 January 1934, 2; *Πρωινή*, 13 January 1934, 4. The first reports in the British newspapers appeared in *The Times*, 15 January 1934, 11.

home (on the corner of Evagoras and Larnaca Avenues)⁵ with Coureas, and Triantafyllides entered his property to find an unknown young man greet him with '*καλησπέρα σας κ. Τριανταφυλλίδη*' (Good evening, Mr Triantafyllides),⁶ before removing a revolver and shooting him twice (one misfired), with one bullet hitting the left side of his abdomen. Triantafyllides was initially attended by Theodoros Artemis and Byron Shakallis before being transferred to the clinic of Dr Miltiades Coureas (a cousin of Nicholas S. Coureas), where doctors Stelios G. Papadopoulos (the government surgeon), Sophocles Lysandrides and Dervis also attended. No bullet could be found, even after X-rays. Transferred to the Nicosia General Hospital, Dr Papadopoulos performed emergency surgery to extract the bullet and Triantafyllides was given blood. The editors of all three major newspapers expressed their hope that Triantafyllides would recover. Meanwhile, as for the assailant, the shots were heard by Nicholas S. Coureas, while Triantafyllides exited his yard shouting '*συλλάβετέ τον*' (arrest him). Coureas (and according to *Πρωινή* another man, I. Tsiartziazes, who was never mentioned again) chased the assailant, who threatened Coureas in English with a 'hands up' and that he would shoot him too if he did not stop chasing him, before running down Larnaca Avenue towards a hidden bicycle and making for the St Spyridon cemetery. Coureas claimed that the man was about 22. *Πρωινή* revealed that all police resources were devoted to finding the assailant and that the motive was unknown. *Φωνή της Κύπρου* had information that three days before being shot Triantafyllides had given police an anonymous letter threatening him and that at 10 p.m. Georgios Eleftheriou Xia had been held, although later released. The articles used elevated language in reaction to the shooting, such as 'brazen', 'disgusting' and 'atrocious', which had 'shocked' and 'upset' the community and which *Πρωινή* stated 'constituted a barbaric act of primitive instincts'.⁷

Triantafyllides died at 5:45 a.m. on 13 January (see Figure 2.1 for one of the many photos published in the newspapers). His funeral was held at the Church of Archangel Michael (known as Tripiotis) the next day at 10 a.m., officiated by the *Locum Tenens*, Leontios.⁸ As previously stated, Leontios did not deliver a eulogy or attend the burial, both acts being highly unusual, controversial and suspicious.⁹ During the ten days following his death most newspapers commented on the assassination. The editors mostly paid tribute to Triantafyllides. Fasouliotis of *Παρατηρητής* was heartbroken, claiming

---

⁵ Larnaca Avenue is today Makariou Avenue.
⁶ *Ελευθερία*, 13 January 1934, 3; *Νέος Κυπριακός Φύλαξ*, 17 January 1934, 2.
⁷ *Ελευθερία*, 13 January 1934, 3; *Φωνή της Κύπρου*, 13 January 1934, 2; *Πρωινή*, 13 January 1934, 4; *Πρωινή*, 14 January 1934, 4.
⁸ *Πρωινή*, 14 January 1934, 4.
⁹ FCO141/2464, secret, Hart-Davis to Henniker-Heaton, 14 April 1934.

Figure 2.1 Antonios Triantafyllides, Vassiliou Studio, Limassol, 1928. Photo appeared in *Φωνή της Κύπρου*, 20 January 1934.

Source: Courtesy of Stelios A. Triantafyllides, Nicosia, Cyprus.

that this was a tragedy for Cyprus and that Triantafyllides had much more to offer his country.[10] *Πρωινή* echoed this language and tone, adding that he was 'much loved'.[11] *Φωνή της Κύπρου* also praised him: 'He was gifted with enviable mental and spiritual charisma [...] and attention to detail'.[12] *Νέος Κυπριακός Φύλαξ* and *Ελευθερία* were more guarded in their praise. The former commended his lawyering skills but said nothing about his role in politics; while the latter acknowledged that it did not always agree with Triantafyllides's political decisions, namely him joining the advisory council.[13]

---

[10] *Παρατηρητής*, 14 January 1934, 6.
[11] *Πρωινή*, 15 January 1934, 4. Also, the editor commented that Triantafyllides was too educated to predict that there was someone so primitive as to assassinate him. *Πρωινή*, 19 January 1934, 2.
[12] *Φωνή της Κύπρου*, 20 January 1934, 2.
[13] *Νέος Κυπριακός Φύλαξ*, 17 January 1934, 2; *Ελευθερία*, 17 January 1934, 2.

There were thousands at the funeral and hundreds at memorial services across the island. Rupert Gunnis, Inspector of Antiquities, commented that at the funeral there were 'thousands of people, I never saw such crowds'.[14] The Colonial Secretary, Herbert Henniker-Heaton (another Australian by birth), represented Governor Herbert Richmond Palmer (who had replaced Stubbs in November 1933), and was joined by the Chief Judge Sir Herbert Strong; the judges in the Supreme Court, Basil Sertsios and Fuad Bey; the district commissioner of Nicosia, Charles Hart-Davis; the Attorney General, Henry Blackall; the Deputy Crown Prosecutor and Solicitor General, Neoptolemos Paschalis; the president of the Nicosia district court, Charles Abbot; and his judges Stavros E. Stavrinides, Raif Mehmet Bey, Menelaos Melissas, Sophocles Tingiris and Petros Anastasiades; and many other dignitaries. Ioannis Clerides gave a moving eulogy, praising Triantafyllides for his contribution to society and public life, for his exceptional lawyering skills and his wise political views and advice.[15] Several newspapers documented the memorial held at 11 a.m. on the morning of his death at the district law courts in Nicosia, where numerous colleagues and friends praised his lawyering abilities and friendship, including Abbot, the secretary of the Bar, Nicholas G. Chrysafinis, and the district court judges Petros Anastasiades and Raif Mehmet Bey.[16] The latter, tellingly for a Cypriot Muslim who may be considered antipathetic to Greek Cypriots (and is the father of the nationalist Turkish Cypriot politician and leader Rauf Raif Denktaş), asserted that Triantafyllides was 'not only a first-rate lawyer but a capable politician', thus reflecting the fact that Triantafyllides was sensitive of Turkish Cypriot views.[17] The legal fraternity were united in their grief at memorials in Limassol (14 January), where Criton G. Tornaritis, later Attorney General in British Cyprus (1952–56) and the Republic of Cyprus (1960–84), gave a poignant speech,[18] Famagusta (16 January) and Larnaca (18 January), with Stelios Pavlides attending, with Strong going to the Larnaca service.[19] Given the many hundreds attending, there was a major outpouring of affection from across Cypriot society, particularly the educated classes, and especially the legal community, as well as a deep sense of shock that this happened in Cyprus.

---

[14] *Costas and Rita Severis Foundation: Centre of Visual Arts and Research* (hereafter CVAR) ARF/01092, Diary of Rupert Gunnis, 14 January 1934.
[15] *Ελευθερία*, 17 January 1934, 2.
[16] See *Πρωινή*, 14 January 1934, 4; *Ελευθερία*, 17 January 1934, 2.
[17] *Πρωινή*, 14 January 1934, 4.
[18] *Αλήθεια*, 19 January 1934, 2.
[19] *Ελευθερία*, 20 January 1934, 3; *Πρωινή*, 18 January 1934, 4.

The newspapers reported that the police were actively involved in finding the culprit, but gave little detail. On 17 January, newspapers reported that several people had been arrested in connection with the assassination of Triantafyllides and that the police had questioned countless others. Meanwhile, they announced, rather casually, that five men had been taken from Nicosia to remote places in Cyprus and placed under house arrest: George Markides, a lawyer and former mayor of Nicosia, taken to Peristerona, Paphos; Dr Pigasiou, taken to Agios Nicholas, Paphos; Pygmalion Ioannides, a lawyer, taken to Galatarka, Paphos; Polycarpos Ioannides, the secretary of the Kyrenia Diocese, to Kellaki, Limassol; and Evagoras Papa Nicolaou, a lawyer and editor of *Πρωτεύουσα*, to Androlikou, Paphos.[20] No further detail was given. Then in March and May, the newspapers reported that one of them, Dr Pigasiou, had been given leave to temporarily return to Nicosia, the first time to perform an operation and the second for a court case.[21]

There are many important points to draw from the evidence in the newspapers. Nicholas S. Coureas was the most important witness, since he was the only person alive that had seen and been spoken to by the assassin. It would therefore be logical that he would play an important part in the police investigation and any prosecution case. The newspapers did not discuss motives, let alone political motives, perhaps because of censorship, or because the editors were in shock or unwilling to speculate, or because they knew who was really behind it, especially after the internment of the five. Interestingly, unlike the theory of a communist conspiracy, which the British took to court 12 months later, the anti-communist newspapers did not attribute the shooting to the communists and never did. The newspapers oscillated between strong and guarded praise for Triantafyllides, with some criticism of his political actions, yet no attack on his character, as will be shown there was in the Athenian press. If popularity could be measured by the number attending your funeral and memorial – in this case, island-wide memorials – then Triantafyllides was popular with many ordinary Cypriots. *Πρωινή* was particularly strong in its praise, referring to Triantafyllides as the most ablest, intelligent and spirited politician on the island, and the only one with any serious national and international profile.[22] One person, K. Nicolaou from Xeros, Nicosia, told Palmer that Triantafyllides was 'ever memorable', his wife, children and 'the whole of Cyprus', were mourning because he was a 'good advocate and politician'. The government too, Nicolaou believed, would be mourning his loss because he

---

[20] *Χρόνος*, 17 January 1934, 4; *Ελευθερία*, 17 January 1934, 3.
[21] *Φωνή της Κύπρου*, 31 March 1934, 3; *Πρωινή*, 5 May 1934, 4.
[22] *Πρωινή*, 19 January 1934, 2.

was 'good and honest' in trying to work with it 'for the progress and advancement of this unfortunate people'. He begged Palmer only 'that the assassin should meet death the same way as the victim', which would 'deter other people possessed of the same felonious instincts'.[23]

The Proceedings against Stavros Christodoulou

A year to the day of the shooting, Stavros Christodoulou, a 22-year-old born in Kato Dikomo, Kyrenia, appeared before the president of the Nicosia district court, Charles Abbot, accused of assassinating Triantafyllides.[24] Christodoulou, described as small statured, with a narrow forehead, joined eyebrows, and a nervous disposition, was already serving life (convicted in November 1934) for the attempted murder in July 1934 of Costas Anastasiades, the mayor of Agios Dometios, a suburb of Nicosia.[25] Christodoulou pleaded not guilty, refused representation and started a hunger strike in protest at the charges. The crown announced that over 30 witnesses would be called, interestingly Nicholas S. Coureas was not one of them.[26]

The inquest started on 21 January and ended on 23 January. The crown was represented by none other than Neoptolemos Paschalis, the long-time associate and friend of Triantafyllides, and the Solicitor General and Deputy Crown Prosecutor. He argued that Christodoulou was part of the criminal underworld and assassinated Triantafyllides for money as part of a communist conspiracy to assassinate leading Cypriots cooperating with the government, or, as *The Times* back in London put it, as part of an act of 'Communist terrorism'.[27] On the day of his shooting, Triantafyllides had been to Larnaca for a case and returned to his Nicosia office at 1:45 p.m., where he had an appointment with a client, Angelos Daskalopoulos. They left with Nicholas S. Coureas for the Gazi Bar, where they had a few glasses of cognac, before Triantafyllides and Coureas left for their homes, which were next to each other.[28]

The fundamental problem for the prosecution was that its own witnesses contradicted their case of a communist conspiracy and implicated a far right pro-*enosis* extremist who had been interned in connection with the assassination. Of the 31 witnesses, several claimed that Christodoulou had admitted

---

[23] FCO141/2497, K. Nicolaou (of Xeros) to Palmer, 17 January 1934.
[24] *Νέος Κυπριακός Φύλαξ*, 13 January 1935, 4; *Χρόνος*, 14 January 1935, 4; *Ελευθερία*, 16 January 1934, 2.
[25] See *Πρωινή*, 14 November 1934, 4; *Ελευθερία*, 23 January 1935, 2.
[26] *Νέος Κυπριακός Φύλαξ*, 13 January 1935, 4; *Ελευθερία*, 16 January 1934, 2.
[27] *The Times*, 24 January 1935, 11.
[28] *Χρόνος*, 23 January 1935, 4; *Πρωινή*, 12 February 1935, 4.

to the murder. One witness, Sotiris Antoniou Mavros, originally from Agios Georgios (near Spathariko), Famagusta, even admitted to being an accessory. Mavros, who had lived with Christodoulou until a month before the assassination and knew him for 3–4 years, testified that Christodoulou had told him that he found a '*κκελεππούρι*' (an easy job), which was £70 from Dr Ioannis Pigasiou to shoot Triantafyllides. Clearly, this was not a part of the prosecution case. Mavros initially refused to help Christodoulou, but then agreed to stand on Larnaca Avenue with a bicycle when offered a cut of the money. On hearing the shots, he saw the accused run from Triantafyllides's house, and presuming he was safe, Mavros rode the bicycle to Christodoulou's lodgings. Christodoulou arrived riding a bicycle without a light, proclaiming that he had shot Triantafyllides after greeting him 'good evening' and proceeding to explain to Mavros that he had known Triantafyllides's movements that day and had followed him after he had left his office. Mavros gave him the other bicycle and left. Mavros, who claimed he had been a communist for a year after the 1931 disturbances, stated that Christodoulou had been a communist then too, but had fallen out with some of them who he subsequently threatened to kill. Christodoulou, Mavros claimed, had also threatened Savvas Loizou and so he had feared speaking to the police about what he knew and his role in the shooting of Triantafyllides. Loizou revealed that he saw Christodoulou enter Triantafyllides's house on the night of the murder, heard the two shots and saw Christodoulou flee. Loizou then saw the accused at Triantafyllides's funeral on Sunday 14 January 1934, when Christodoulou suggested that they get into the photo around the grave, but Loizou refused and blamed him with the crime. Christodoulou then threatened to kill Loizou if he said anything, causing him to become ill from anxiety, exacerbated when the accused brought him a bottle of milk, which contained a black substance at the bottom. Loizou accused Christodoulou of trying to poison him, to which the defendant revealed to Loizou that those who had paid him to kill Triantafyllides had given him the milk. About 15–20 days before the assassination, Loizou saw Christodoulou leaving the house of Dr Pigasiou with money, which he assumed Christodoulou had gotten from a girl working there as he often extorted money from girls upon the promise of marriage. Later at Skouriotissa, where they had gone to find work, Christodoulou claimed that he would go to Nicosia to deal with Pigasiou (released on 2 June 1934),[29] telling Loizou that after doing various jobs for him the doctor saw that Christodoulou was unemployed and offered to pay him handsomely, find him a wife and open a store for him in Nicosia if he killed Triantafyllides. If accused, Pigasiou promised to pay for his legal

---

[29] *Φωνή της Κύπρου*, 2 June 1934, 3.

fees. Christodoulou agreed and Pigasiou made him swear on the Bible (which a communist was unlikely to do).[30] Asked why Pigasiou wanted Triantafyllides assassinated, Loizou claimed that he assumed it was over women and personal animosity, which could be anything, including politics.[31]

These sensational claims continued throughout the pre-hearing. One witness, Therapis Christou, recruited by the police on the night of the shooting because the accused had once worked at his coffee-house at Kaimakli, claimed that Christodoulou had admitted to shooting Triantafyllides when they had spent the night in the same cell. Several *Zaptiehs* (police) were near the Triantafyllides home when the shooting happened, but could not identify the murderer. Lieutenant Savvas Pavlou also read Christodoulou's signed, voluntary statement, given on 3 November 1934, only days before his conviction for attempted murder, which claimed that he had been a communist from 1931 to 1933, but when after he left, he was persecuted by other communists for leaving it. The police also referred to a letter from Christodoulou to Nikos Poullos, his co-accused in the attempted murder of Anastasiades, that stated that Christodoulou had been paid to kill Triantafyllides. Yet in his statement, Christodoulou accused Pantelis Mathaiou, a communist who had proposed the murder of various government officials to make money. It is possible that this statement and that Christodoulou had been a communist had convinced the British authorities of a communist conspiracy, but this evidence is flimsy and comes from the defendant who may have been trying to throw the British off the far right conspiracy. Christodoulou accepted that he had gone with Mathaiou and had therefore been an accessory, but that Mathaiou had shot Triantafyllides. Christodoulou was mixing the events on purpose to confuse the case, since this is likely what happened, but with him pulling the trigger and with Mavros as his accessory. When Mathaiou appeared as a crown witness, he claimed that on the night of the shooting he was at work from 6 to 11 p.m., which was verified by others from his work. He also claimed that it had been Christodoulou who had planned to kill government officials to make money, something corroborated by Demetris Haralambous, who knew the accused for 5–6 years. This was also evident from Christodoulou's earlier conviction for the attempted murder of Anastasiades.[32]

---

[30] Before the formation of AKEL, the Cypriot communists were strongly anti-church, even abusive of it, see FCO141/2455.

[31] *Cyprus Mail*, 22 January 1935, 3; *Πρωινή*, 22 January 1935, 1, 3–4; *Νέος Κυπριακός Φύλαξ*, 22 January 1935, 1, 4; *Cyprus Mail*, 23 January 1935, 3; *Αλήθεια*, 25 January 1935, 2; *Ελευθερία*, 26 January 1935, 4.

[32] *Cyprus Mail*, 23 January 1935, 3; *Νέος Κυπριακός Φύλαξ*, 23 January 1935, 1, 4; *Νέος Κυπριακός Φύλαξ*, 24 January 1935, 1, 4; *Φωνή της Κύπρου*, 26 January 1935, 3; *Ελευθερία*, 26 January 1935, 4.

Abbot decided that there was enough evidence to transfer the case to the criminal court.³³ It opened on 11 February and sat on 12, 14, 15 and 18, until delivering a verdict of not guilty on 25 February. The court went over the same ground as the pre-hearing and the witnesses remained faithful to their previous testimonies. This time there were three judges (Abbot, Strong and Raif Mehmet) and the crown (Paschalis, also the acting Attorney General from 6 February to 19 March while Blackall was on sick leave); and the defendant was represented by Stavros G. Stavrinakis (at the request of Strong), a lawyer since 1904 and an active 'populist', who had served on the legislative (1925–30 and 1930–31) and executive (1926–29) councils.³⁴ The main difference from the pre-hearing was that all three judges could at any time ask the witnesses questions and Stavrinakis could cross-examine them. Paschalis again pushed the communist conspiracy theory and avoided the evidence against Pigasiou and other evidence that contradicted the theory. Stavrinakis and the judges picked holes in the case of the prosecution and questioned several witnesses. The judges pressed the witnesses about why they had not told the police what they knew earlier, and they replied that they reported what they knew as soon as Christodoulou had been arrested in July 1934 for the attempted murder of Anastasiades because they were scared to do so while he was free because Christodoulou might kill them and that they would get into trouble either as accessories or for not coming forward earlier.³⁵ Judge Raif accused Mavros of formulating his testimony on newspaper reports to obtain the controversially introduced £1,000 reward for information leading to a conviction, even though the reward had been available since February 1934. Also, the police had reported that Christodoulou, upon seeing Mavros at the police station, had stated that 'if Sotiris has come here for me, then he will dig my grave', and if that were the case, why would his evidence not have aligned with the prosecution case, and implicated a communist figure?³⁶

---

³³ *Νέος Κυπριακός Φύλαξ*, 24 January 1935, 4.
³⁴ *Ελευθερία*, 7 February 1935, 4; *Cyprus Blue Book for 1935*, CGPO, Nicosia, 1936, 166; *Cyprus Gazette 1935*, British Colonial Government, Nicosia, 1935, 85. Coudounaris, *Βιογραφικόν Λεξικόν Κυπρίων*, 354.
³⁵ *Πρωινή*, 12 February 1935, 1, 4; *Νέος Κυπριακός Φύλαξ*, 12 February 1935, 1, 8; *Κυπριακός Τύπος* (Cypriot Press), 12 February 1935, 1, 4; *Ελευθερία*, 13 February 1935, 2, 4; *Cyprus Mail*, 14 February 1935, 3; *Κυπριακός Τύπος*, 15 February 1935, 1, 4; *Νέος Κυπριακός Φύλαξ*, 15 February 1935, 1, 4; *Πρωινή*, 15 February 1935, 1, 4; *Cyprus Mail*, 16 February 1935, 3; *Ελευθερία*, 16 February 1935, 2, 4; *Πρωινή*, 16 February 1935, 1, 4; *Νέος Κυπριακός Φύλαξ*, 16 February 1935, 1, 4; *Κυπριακός Τύπος*, 16 February 1935, 1, 4; *Cyprus Mail*, 18 February 1935, 3; *Cyprus Mail*, 20 February 1935, 2; *Αλήθεια*, 22 February 1935, 2.
³⁶ *Cyprus Mail*, 14 February 1935, 3. FCO141/2497, Henniker-Heaton to King, 29 January 1934; FCO141/2497, King to Henniker-Heaton, 31 January 1934; FCO141/

The other difference was the testimony of Dr Miltiades Coureas on the circumstances of Triantafyllides's last hours. Dr Coureas stated that soon after leaving the clinic of Dr Marsellos a car stopped in front of his and Triantafyllides got out. He was wounded, so Dr Coureas took him to his clinic, and called Dr Papadopoulos and they decided to locate the bullet with an X-ray machine. After several attempts, the bullet was located. By now it was necessary to operate, and Dr Papadopoulos took Triantafyllides to the General Hospital and in the presence of Dr Coureas operated to tie several cut arteries. They saw the bullet, but since it was not in a precarious place, they left it. The surgery lasted for an hour and finished at 9:30 p.m. By 12:30 a.m., Triantafyllides's condition had improved, but by 3 a.m. he had deteriorated and Dr Coureas called Dr Cyril Cuff, the government surgical specialist, who arrived at 4 a.m. Papadopoulos conducted the autopsy in Cuff's presence, and extracted the bullet. Coureas claimed that he was a close personal friend of Triantafyllides, but did not say if he was his personal physician.[37] In his 2002 interview, Michalakis Triantafyllides claimed that the medical care given to his father was bungled; namely, that the search for the bullet had taken too long and his father had lost too much blood, and then the blood they gave him was the wrong group. He claimed that the British government surgeon was not in Cyprus at the time, when in fact Dr Cuff was in Nicosia, but only attended his father at 4 a.m. Although Michalakis does not say if Dr Coureas was his father's personal physician or the one who pulled his name from the hat, he implied that he and Dr Papadopoulos were either negligent, inexperienced or involved in the conspiracy.[38] One cannot rule this out, since Dr Coureas had opportunity, and as will be shown later, he played an active role in the far right after the Second World War, even though he had signed a declaration in 1922.[39]

2497, Reward Notice, undated. On 29 January Henniker-Heaton asked King for his view on offering a reward for information that would lead to an arrest. King advised that a reward was usually offered if the accused was known and so in this case 'a reward for information which may lead to the apprehension and conviction of a man at present unknown, may lead to undesirable results e.g. the fabrication of a complete chain of evidence against an innocent man'. Yet King claimed that 'no great harm can now be done by the offer of a reward' because the police could check information, so a reward was offered, initially £250 (announced *Πρωινή*, 4 February 1934, 4), later increased to £1,000.

[37] *Κυπριακός Τύπος*, 20 February 1935, 4; *Νέος Κυπριακός Φύλαξ*, 20 February 1935, 4.
[38] Michalakis Triantafyllides interview, 1 February 2002, in Solomonidou-Drousiotou, *Η Ζωή μου σε Πρώτο Πρόσωπο*, 33–41.
[39] Varnava, *British Cyprus and the Long Great War*, 199.

In the end, Strong and Raif delivered a verdict of not guilty, but Abbot abstained (contrary to what Michalakis said in his interview). Strong and Raif believed that the crown had failed to prove Christodoulou's guilt, while Abbot was unsure. The court argued that the crown's witnesses were unreliable, especially Mavros, whose testimony, even according to Paschalis, needed significant reinforcement to be believed. The judges questioned why Mavros had never asked Christodoulou why Pigasiou would want to pay to kill Triantafyllides, something that Mavros did not initially believe because he did not believe that a man like Pigasiou would speak to Christodoulou, yet he found out later that the accused had worked for Pigasiou.[40]

The judges were damning of the police investigation and crown case, and Paschalis acknowledged that the evidence was weak. But there were more problems with the case if one reads the evidence against the grain. First, the crown did not properly explain the testimony of Therapis Christou, whom the police placed in a cell with Christodoulou on the night of the shooting. If Christodoulou had confessed on that night, why had Christou not told the police, or if he had, why had the police released Christodoulou? A major omission was the crown not calling Nicholas S. Coureas, the only witness to have confronted the shooter. Coureas had made a statement to police after the shooting and stood before a line-up of suspects, including Christodoulou, but was not called by the prosecution because, as the police reported to the government and as his grandson (and namesake), historian Dr Nicholas Coureas, also confirmed, he had identified several suspects as the potential shooter, thus making him an unreliable witness.[41] Stavrinakis drew attention to his absence, raising questions about the prosecution case: if the main witness could not identify the killer, how could anyone be found guilty without an admission? Christodoulou's behaviour, especially in comparison to his earlier trial for attempted murder, was also important. He had pleaded guilty to the attempted murder of Anastasiades, yet claimed to have been hypnotised by the second accused (Nikos Poullos, who was sentenced to 20 years).[42] In the Triantafyllides case he accused the witnesses of having a 'talent for myth-making' and of belonging to a police set-up, protesting with his hunger strike and by initially refusing representation. Such behaviour hints at acting to stave off execution. There is no doubt that Christodoulou was violent, he had been charged with attempted murder of a fellow prisoner in 1936,[43]

---

[40] *Cyprus Mail*, 26 February 1935, 2; *Κυπριακός Τύπος*, 26 February 1935, 1, 4; *Πρωινή*, 16 February 1935, 1, 4.

[41] FCO141/2497, King to Henniker-Heaton, 13 January 1934; Nicholas Coureas, email to author, 15 September 2016.

[42] *Πρωινή*, 14 November 1934, 4; *Αλήθεια*, 18 January 1935, 2.

[43] *Cyprus Mail*, 27 April 1936, 2.

and given the evidence had likely shot Triantafyllides. Yet, ultimately, as will be explored in the next chapter, whoever pulled the trigger was doing so as the hired gun of others.

The other anomaly was the prosecution avoiding the evidence of several witnesses implicating Pigasiou and the flimsy evidence, which was contradicted by their own witnesses, of a communist conspiracy. Usually, the prosecution prepares their witnesses to give evidence, but clearly, in this case, several witnesses went off script, implicating a pro-*enosis* fanatic, indicating that their evidence was believable. Pigasiou was the head of the Pancyprian League of Volunteers to the Greek Wars, so fanatical that Storrs had wanted him deported (in a second round of deportations) after the 1931 riots, but he was instead interned until 1933. Pigasiou had studied medicine in Athens, volunteered in the Balkan Wars of 1912–13, and later served as a doctor in Epirus during the Greek revolt there in 1914. Returning to Cyprus in 1915, he practised as a surgeon in Karavas, Kyrenia, and in Nicosia, was involved in nationalist politics, and became a far right extremist.[44] Pigasiou was a member of EREK, with Loizides, Polycarpos Ioannides and Papa Nicolaou. Loizides, as discussed earlier, was the leading figure in EREK which was backed by the finances of the Kyrenia Bishopric. He was deported, along with Bishop Makarios, after the 1931 riots and settled in Athens to lead the Cyprus 'political bureau' with Makarios.[45] He was notorious for his violent attacks on anyone who wavered in their advocacy of *enosis* or worked for, or, with the British, including on Triantafyllides after he had joined the executive council. Loizides was linked to Christodoulou because both were from Kato Dikomo, Kyrenia. He had given the name of National Radical Union of Cyprus (EREK), which had weapons concealed for use against any leading persons cooperating with the British.[46] As will be shown in the next chapter, the British and others were from the beginning convinced of a connection with Athens.

---

[44] Georghallides, *Cyprus and the Governorship of Sir Ronald Storrs*, 353, 414–17, 592, 607, 619, 706; Coudounaris, *Βιογραφικόν Λεξικόν Κυπρίων*, 306; Petros Papapolyviou (ed. & intro.), *Υπόδουλοι Ελευθερωταί Αδελφών Αλυτρώτων: Πολεμικά Ημερολόγια, Επιστολές και Ανταποκρίσεις Κυπρίων Εθελοντών από την Ήπειρο και τη Μακεδονία του 1912–1913* [Enslaved Free Brother Soldiers: War Diaries, Letters and Responses of Cypriot Volunteers from Epirus and Macedonia 1912–1913] (Nicosia: Cyprus Research Centre, 1999), 200–81.

[45] For the arrests of Makarios and Loizides in October 1931, see *Evening Telegraph*, 27 October 1931, 5.

[46] Loizides, *Άτυχη Κύπρος*, 22–29, 37, 73; Chrysanthis, 'Ιστορικά Δεδομένα σχετικά με το κίνημα του 1931', 451–56; Georghallides, *Cyprus and the Governorship of Sir Ronald Storrs*, 408, 414–17, 600–602, 642–43, 685.

Had the prosecution put forward a far right conspiracy to assassinate Triantafyllides, with three witnesses saying that Christodoulou had admitted to the shooting and that he was paid by Pigasiou, it is highly likely that all three judges would have returned a guilty verdict. Given the evidence implicating Pigasiou, it is surprising that the British authorities developed the communist conspiracy theory, reflecting their unhealthy anti-communist obsession in Cyprus.[47] However, as the evidence from the colonial archive will show in the next chapter, the British authorities initially believed that the conspiracy to assassinate Triantafyllides emanated from pro-*enosis* extremists in Cyprus with connections to those deported in Athens, where they were clamouring in favour of *enosis*, using the finances of the Kyrenia Bishopric and the Athenian newspapers. It is therefore surprising that the British authorities dropped this line of conspiracy, which their witnesses supported, for one which they contradicted.

---

[47] See FCO141/2455.

Chapter 3

THE COLONIAL GOVERNMENT ARCHIVE AND THE TRIANTAFYLLIDES CASE

> Some months ago Savvas Loizides, Theodoros Kolokasides and Theophanis Tsangarides proposed to me (Bishop Nicodemos) to try to go to Athens for the purpose of taking presidency of an association whose aim was to use all means, murders not excluded, against those Cypriots who co-operate with the Government.
>
> Theophanis Theodotou to Philip Cunliffe-Lister, 26 January 1934.

On 12 January 1934, Henry Blackall, the Attorney General since 1932, gave notice of his intention to marry Maria Severis, daughter of Demosthenis Severis and first cousin of Loulla Triantafyllides, Antonios's wife, in the Orthodox Church (which happened on 21 April 1934). But that night he returned to his diary (noticeable by the darker ink) to enter the details of what was then 'an attempt to assassinate Triantafyllides'. Blackall rang and then visited the General Hospital where Triantafyllides was being operated on. One shot had entered the intestines, which were perforated in four places, and the 'doctors regard his condition as very serious, but there is [...] some hope'. His immediate view was that this was 'the first political assassination here and it is doubtless owed to the poison instilled by the local press', and therefore 'censorship should be revived'. Blackall noted that Triantafyllides had 'helped a lot towards our engagement'.[1] The next day, Blackall entered the death of Triantafyllides and how he influenced the immediate actions of Governor Palmer (Figure 3.1).

---

[1] CVAR, ARF/00284, Diary of Sir Henry Blackall, 12 January 1934. Coincidentally, my wife and I share the same wedding anniversary as Henry and Maria Blackall, 73 years later.

Figure 3.1 Sir Herbert Richmond Palmer, 1924.

Source: Family Archives licensed under the Creative Commons Attribution-Share Alike 3.0.

> On going to see Henniker-Heaton (Col Sec) I found that he pooh-poohed the idea that it was a political murder. As I disagreed, I went to see the Governor with Paschalis (S-G) and had no difficulty in convincing him that it was. Paschalis believes that it was instigated by the irreconcilable clique who are at the back of all trouble here including the intransigence of the Archb (Archbishop, i.e. *Locum Tenens*, Bishop Leontios). So I advised His Excellency to intern the leaders of the clique.[2]

Palmer agreed and also called a company of troops from Limassol to Nicosia, which Blackall disagreed with because

> Most of us are against this as public opinion seems to be entirely against the murder and no trouble need therefore be anticipated while the presence of troops may be resented as uncalled for.[3]

---

[2] Ibid., 13 January 1934.
[3] Ibid.

Meanwhile, in Athens, Savvas Loizides, Bishop Makarios, Theophanis Tsangarides and Theodoros Kolokasides must have received the news that Triantafyllides had died with a mixture of excitement and apprehension. After the arrest and internment of their colleagues in Cyprus, their apprehension would have grown. At that point, the right-wing Athenian newspapers published several articles and editorials, influenced by or emanating from the exiles there, which asserted that the assassination was motivated by personal vengeance, thus creating the personal motive theory that entered Cypriot national consciousness.

The evidence in the colonial archive, however, supports the theory of a far right conspiracy to assassinate Triantafyllides. This was the gut feeling of Blackall, Paschalis and Palmer, who took quick action to intern five of them. The evidence in the archive points to some of them being the co-conspirators of colleagues in Athens. Telling evidence comes from letters by Theophanis Theodotou, Triantafyllides's father-in-law, a deportee in London, and another from Brewster Joseph Surridge, the District Commissioner of Larnaca. Both believed that the deportees in Athens were behind the assassination.

Palmer immediately telegraphed the Secretary of State Cunliffe-Lister, early on 13 January with the news of the assassination and his actions to bring troops to Nicosia and, as Blackall advised, to intern five extremists opposed to Triantafyllides and restore press censorship.[4] These actions reflected Triantafyllides's importance to the government and Cunliffe-Lister approved.[5] A platoon of troops was moved to Nicosia from Limassol on 13 January and a company, less one platoon, was moved on 16 January, thus, altogether, one company of troops was moved to Nicosia.[6] Palmer told Cunliffe-Lister on 17 January that there might be 'a personal side' to the murder, but 'the political effect is inescapable', with the Mayor of Nicosia, Dr Dervis, 'in a state of panic, so were the Cypriot Government Officials'. Therefore, he ordered on 13 January the internment in isolated rural villages of five far right pro-*enosis* nationalists from Nicosia, as they had viciously attacked Triantafyllides in the newspapers. They were those listed in the newspapers on 17 January: George

---

[4] FCO141/2497, telegram, immediate, Palmer to Cunliffe-Lister, 13 January 1934. The Colonial Office immediately informed the Foreign Office, FO371/18391/265, immediate, CO to FO, 13 January 1934.
[5] FCO141/2497, telegram, Cunliffe-Lister to Palmer, 13 January 1934. A similar telegram was also sent to the OCTE, who offered to send a staff officer, but Palmer believed this was premature. FCO141/2497, telegram, Palmer to OCTE, of 13 January 1934; FCO141/2497, telegram, Egypt force to Palmer, 14 January 1934; FCO141/2497, telegram, Palmer to Egypt force, 15 January 1934.
[6] CO67/253/10, secret, telegram, OCTE to WO, 16 January 1934.

Markides, the ex-mayor of Nicosia; Evagoras Papa Nicolaou, a lawyer and journalist, who published Bishop Makarios's organ in Nicosia *Πρωτεύουσα*; Pygmalion Ioannides, a lawyer imprisoned after the 1931 disturbances; Polycarpos Stylianou Ioannides, the fanatical secretary of the Kyrenia Bishopric, also imprisoned in 1931 and writer for *Πρωτεύουσα*; and lastly none other than Dr Pigasiou.[7] Papa Nicolaou, Polycarpos Ioannides and Dr Pigasiou were EREK fanatics and signatories to the oath of 18 October, which contributed to the riots, and are lauded by nationalists like Petros Stylianou.[8] The dossier on Pigasiou revealed that he had been particularly active. He was interned after the October 1931 riots until April 1933 and only released after signing a declaration that he would not be involved in politics, but continued his activities with the other fanatical friends of Bishop Makarios and Loizides.[9] Palmer claimed that the banishment of these five had restored morale, 'but as several more members have been threatened, there is a definite chance of a repetition'. He urged London to relieve the tension by appointing a committee of financial experts to report on the economy, to 'take the wind out of the sails of the Enosis people'.[10]

Palmer also revealed that Triantafyllides had claimed that his shooting was political. There was still no evidence

> [...] as to whether the murder was purely political in origin or not, but there is no doubt that the act will be treated by those hostile to British rule here and in Greece as the outcome of oppressive rule.

The attacks on Triantafyllides for joining the advisory council were 'bitter and inciting in tone', according to Palmer's assessment of the newspapers, and that

> [...] the crime is of utmost concern to the Government as Mr Triantafyllides was the leading figure among the 'National' politicians

---

[7] SA1/438/34, minute, Attorney General, 13 January 1934; Defence of Cyprus (Consolidation and Amendment No. 2) Regulations, 1931; SA1/438/34, order, signed Palmer and Henniker-Heaton, 13 January 1934; SA1/438/34, CSC to CCPC, 15 January 1934; CO67/253/10, secret, Palmer to Cunliffe-Lister, 19 January 1934, including enclosures, dossiers on Markides, Papa Nicolaou, Pygmalion Ioannides, Polycarpos Ioannides and Pigasiou.

[8] Stylianou, *Το Κίνημα του Οκτώβρη του 1931 στην Κύπρο*, 57–58; For an English translation, see Jan Asmussen, 'Disturbances in Cyprus in October, 1931', *Journal of Cyprus Studies* 12 (2006): 5–55.

[9] CO67/253/10, secret, Palmer to Cunliffe-Lister, 19 January 1934, enclosure, dossier on Pigasiou.

[10] CO67/253/10, secret, Palmer to Parkinson, 17 January 1934.

who by advocating the policy of co-operation with the Government incurred the hatred of extremists.

Since the 1931 events, Palmer argued that there remained in Nicosia 'a camarilla of extremists which has been a focus of danger', retaining power by controlling the Kyrenia Diocese and would have benefitted from the assassination were it not for their banishment.[11] The British authorities believed that they had several motives to assassinate Triantafyllides. Their dossiers revealed that they were all dangerous because they openly carried out their *enosis* propaganda, had opposed Triantafyllides joining the advisory council (and its formation) and his view that the deported bishops should resign to facilitate the election of a new archbishop.[12]

The death of Archbishop Kyrillos III in November 1933 had left a vacancy of the archiepiscopal throne. According to canon law, the Bishop of Paphos, Leontios, the most senior bishop, became *Locum Tenens*, and should issue a circular for a new election within 15 days. But because Makarios and Nicodemos were deported and not permitted to return, he sought advice 'from eminent lawyers'. Amongst them must be counted Triantafyllides and Ioannis Clerides. They advised that 'the deportation of the two members of the Synod does not legally constitute a justification for the postponement of the election'. On 21 November 1933, Leontios hinted at taking the legal advice and issuing the election circular by the deadline of 30 November, thus, to proceed with the election without the two deported bishops, but made the mistake of asking them to wire their views.[13] Contrary to the legal advice, Makarios replied that 'according to the rules', the election was 'absolutely impossible' owing to 'absence of Synod', so a postponement was 'correct'.[14] To ensure that all

---

[11] CO67/253/10, secret, Palmer to Cunliffe-Lister, 19 January 1934, including dossiers.
[12] Ibid.
[13] FCO141/2482, secret, McLaughlan to CSC, 22 November 1933, with extracts from Leontios to Makarios and Nicodemos, 21 November 1933. Paschalis had already pronounced in January 1932 that the presence of the two deported bishops was unnecessary to form a Synod, and that there were numerous options open to form a Synod, such as appointing abbots from monasteries in order of seniority, or bishops from neighbouring churches. CO67/243, Storrs to Cunliffe-Lister, 27 January 1932, enclosing minute, Paschalis, 25 January 1932.
[14] FCO141/2482, secret, CCCP to CSC, 27 November 1933, with extract from telegram, Makarios to Leontios, received 27 November 1933. Nicodemos replied two days later stating that 'presence of Synod is indispensable, suggest postponement'. FCO141/2482, secret, CCCP to CSC, 29 November 1933, including telegram, Nicodemos to Leontios, 29 November 1933.

knew his views, Makarios gave an interview on 27 November in the Athenian newspaper *Πρωία* (Morning), which Patrick Ramsay, the British Ambassador to Greece had described in 1931 as 'the anti-British petty satrap of Cyprus', in which he rejected the formation of a Synod without Nicodemos and himself.[15] The newspapers in Athens, under the influence of Makarios and the other deportees, attacked the Cypriot government for 'persecuting' the Cypriot Church.[16] Such emotion was contradicted by the Bishop of Siatissas in Greece, an expert on Canon Law, who opined via the Reverend Ierotheos Kykkotis to Stavrinides, the editor of *Ελευθερία*, that the problem originated from when the two bishops were deported because the retention of their roles was 'out of place', and since the basic principle of all sacred canons was that flocks should not remain without a shepherd.[17] Kykkotis revealed that when Makarios saw this opinion he demanded the author's head 'be brought to him on a salver' and when he was told to step aside in favour of Nicodemos, the suggestion 'literally enraged him'.[18] Stavrinides asked Kykkotis to contact Christos Androutsos, an authority on Canon Law, for another opinion.[19] But he too agreed that the election could be held without the two deported bishops, as did Photios II, the Ecumenical Patriarch.[20] This was the well-known view of Triantafyllides, popular across the island, particularly with the editors of *Χρόνος, Πάφος* and *Ελευθερία*, and with Dervis, even after Triantafyllides was

---

[15] FCO141/2482, secret, McLaughlan to CSC, 28 November 1933, with extracts from Makarios interview; FO371/15236, Ramsay to Simon, 20 November 1931.

[16] FCO141/2482, British Legation Athens to Sir John Simon, Foreign Secretary, 30 November 1933, with articles on 28 November 1933 in *Έστια* (Focus), on 29 November in *Πρωία, Έστια, Καθημερινή* (Everyday), and on 30 November in *Ελεύθερον Βήμα* (Free Tribune).

[17] FCO141/2482, secret, McLaughlan to CSC, 13 December 1933, enclosing, Kykkotis to Stavrinides, providing report by the Bishop of Siatissis, member of the Church of Greece, 29 November 1933.

[18] FCO141/2482, secret, McLaughlan to CSC, 13 December 1933, enclosing, Kykkotis to Stavrinides, 6 December 1933; FCO141/2482, secret, McLaughlan to CSC, 4 January 1934, enclosing, Kykkotis to Stavrinides, 28 December 1933. Meanwhile, Bishop Nicodemos, in a more measured tone, also rejected the idea that an election could be held without Makarios and himself present, see FCO141/2482, secret, McLaughlan to CSC, 4 January 1934, enclosing, Nicodemos to Leontios, 31 December 1933.

[19] FCO141/2482, secret, McLaughlan to CSC, 16 December 1933, translating, Stavrinides to Metaxakis, 15 December 1933; FCO141/2482, secret, McLaughlan to CSC, 7 February 1934, enclosing, Kykkotis to Stavrinides, 2 February 1934.

[20] FCO141/2482, secret, McLaughlan to CSC, 7 February 1934, enclosing, Kykkotis to Stavrinides, 2 February 1934; FCO141/2482, secret, McLaughlan to CSC, 12 December 1933, with Ch. Economides to Leontios, 9 December 1933.

assassinated.²¹ Thus, Palmer believed, 'the Archiepiscopal question should not be eliminated as a possible motive for the assassination' and was 'satisfied that the most authoritative legal opinion both local and Greek is right in holding that a valid election can be held in the absence of these particular bishops'.²²

While Palmer checked the extremists and introduced measures to convince leading Cypriots to cooperate with the British authorities, the police updated him on their investigations. The Chief Commandant of Police, William King, had reported verbally to Palmer late on 12 January about the shooting. On the next day, he informed Palmer that Triantafyllides had left his office with Mr Daskalopoulos and Nicholas S. Coureas for a bar/hotel in Ledra St, and after a short stay, Triantafyllides and Coureas walked home, parting at the junction (Evagoras and Larnaca Avenues). Two shots were fired and two men exited the property of Triantafyllides, first the perpetrator, who ran down Larnaca Avenue, and then Triantafyllides. Coureas heard the shots and chased the perpetrator, but was threatened with the revolver and told in English to 'stop'. The assassin, who grabbed a bicycle and rode towards the cemetery, was well dressed and well-spoken. C. N. Xiou was arrested for possessing a bicycle with the same tyre marks as that found where the assassin picked up his bicycle. King revealed that only two people could identify the assailant, the deceased and Coureas. Triantafyllides had stated that he did not know his assailant, while Coureas had given two different descriptions of the man, 'which make our task more difficult'. King argued that 'the motive for the murder is not yet established, though believed to be political, and stated by the deceased in his belief to be political'.²³ On Monday, King updated Palmer again on exhaustive police investigations over the weekend, but 'no evidence of any real value has come to light'. Many suspects were interviewed and paraded before witnesses: Xiou was released after not being identified by witnesses. King argued that the police were 'handicapped in their investigation by the absence of reliable evidence pointing definitely to the motive'.²⁴

---

²¹ FCO141/2482, secret, telegram, Palmer to Cunliffe-Lister, 20 February 1934. Alexis Rappas, 'Leondios and the Archiepiscopal Question, 1933–47: The Demise of an Apolitical *Ethnarchy*?', in Varnava and Michael (eds), *The Archbishops of Cyprus in the Modern Age*, 211–39, 217–18.

²² CO67/253/10, secret, Palmer to Cunliffe-Lister, 19 January 1934; FCO141/2482, telegram, Palmer to Cunliffe-Lister, 25 December 1933.

²³ Palmer received several newspaper reports on the shooting. See FCO141/2497, anonymous to Henniker-Heaton, 13 January 1934; FCO141/2497, translation, *Φωνή της Κύπρου*, 13 January 1934; FCO141/2497, translation, *Πρωινή*, 13 January 1934. FCO141/2497, King to Henniker-Heaton, 13 January 1934.

²⁴ FCO141/2497, King to Henniker-Heaton, 15 January 1934.

Ten days after the shooting, King informed Palmer that 'practically the entire personnel of the Nicosia Police and Criminal Investigation Department have been employed', but no valuable information was forthcoming. Late on 17 January King reconstructed the crime, which clarified some matters, but also made the question of identification, should a suspect be charged, difficult because of the darkness. King accepted that the assailant was a Cypriot because he used an expression when fleeing that only a Cypriot would.[25] The police were clearly running in circles.[26]

The British authorities placed too much credence in the comments in Athenian newspapers on the assassination. The attacks in Athenian newspapers on the Cypriot government were periodic from 1931, but increased in late 1933 with the creation of the advisory council. The Cypriot government considered the articles as outrageous propaganda, as they made erroneous claims, such as that the British were committing atrocities against Greek Cypriot nationalists and were planning to settle Jews to reduce the Greek element. Cypriots had debated the settlement of Jews and Triantafyllides probably upset his extremist, anti-Semitic critics, by suggesting that some Jews could be settled if they were experienced industrialists or agriculturalists.[27] The British Ambassador in Athens, Sir Sydney Waterlow, approached the Greek Conservative government's (i.e. People's Party) foreign minister, Demetrios Maximos, who responded that the press was free. But Waterlow reminded Maximos that Greek law made insulting a foreign government punishable by fine or imprisonment, and was used to prosecute a journalist for publishing translations from a book criticising Hitler, thus betraying the government's pro-Nazi sympathies.[28] The articles on Cyprus coincided

---

[25] FCO141/2497, King to Henniker-Heaton, 22 January 1934.

[26] One lead pursued were the actions of the Crown Counsel, Stelios Pavlides, married to Maria, the sister of Loulla, Triantafyllides's wife. On the morning of 13 January, Pavlides instructed the *muhtar* of the quarter to go with him to break the police seals on the door to Triantafyllides's office. Pavlides removed documents, before resealing the door. Pavlides explained that it was Triantafyllides's wish that he destroy personal documents unconnected to the crime. The police corroborated that the documents were unconnected. FCO141/2497, Henniker-Heaton to Pavlides, 22 January 1934; FCO141/2497, Pavlides to Henniker-Heaton, 24 January 1934.

[27] For Triantafyllides's views, see Κυπριακός Τύπος (Cypriot Press), 8 February 1935, 3. Successive British governments rejected settling Jews from Nazi Germany when proposed in the Commons, especially by Josiah Wedgewood. Stavros Panteli, *Place of Refuge: The History of the Jews in Cyprus* (London: Elliott & Thompson, 2003), 109–16.

[28] FO371/18391/102, Waterlow to Simon, 30 December 1933; Ibid., enclosure, summary of articles in Ανεξαρτιτός (Independent); Ibid., enclosure, abridged translation of article in Εστια, 21 December 1933; FO371/18391/525, Palmer to British

with the settlement in Athens of most of the deportees, with intelligence confirming to the Foreign Office and the Egyptian and Cypriot authorities that Bishop Makarios and Loizides had established in Koraes St a 'political bureau' to spread pro-*enosis* and anti-British propaganda.[29] Loizides, who was bitter over the death of his brother Loizos (his body was found in the sea on 29 October 1931), which he blamed on the British, discussed in his memoirs that the 'Cypriot National Bureau' worked with right-wing Greek newspapers and journalists to promote *enosis* and attack the Cypriot government and Cypriots working for/with it.[30] That the exiles were behind these articles was evident from the branding as 'national traitors' of the Cypriots working for the government, namely Paschalis and Pavlides, as Loizides and his friends had done before being deported.[31]

Triantafyllides was similarly abused after his assassination, as the deportees used the Athenian press to claim that his death was not political in trying to show that the British authorities were too eager to blame their colleagues in Cyprus so they could reintroduce repressive measures. A week after the shooting, Palmer informed the Colonial Office that he was

> creditably informed that certain members of the Greek Government are personally mixing themselves up in these intrigues, and it is thought by some that the manner of the murder was unlike that of a Cypriot i.e. that the murderer was sent from Greece.[32]

Palmer repeated this assertion on 24 January, revealing, 'we have sent a code wire to the Minister at Athens asking for details about a certain suspect who belongs to the [Metaxas] "Youth Organisation" mentioned in MI5

Legation, Athens, 3 January 1934; FO371/18391/223, Harold Allen, CO, to E. H. Carr, 11 January 1934; FO371/18391/223, confidential, Allen to Palmer, 11 January 1934; CO67/255/12, Waterlow, 15 February 1934; FO371/18391/1801, Waterlow to Simon, 17 March 1934; FO371/18391/1801, Waterlow to Simon, 17 March 1934, enclosure summary of Λαϊκός Αγών (Popular Struggle) article; CO67/254/5, secret, Palmer to Cunliffe-Lister, 21 March 1934; Ibid., enclosure, telegram, British Minister, Athens to Palmer, 2 March 1934.

[29] FO141/716, secret, political situation in Cyprus, October 1934–April 1935; FO371/18391/525, Waterlow to Palmer, 19 January 1934.

[30] Loizides, Άτυχη Κύπρος, 36, 45–46.

[31] FO371/18391/102, Waterlow to Simon, 30 December 1933, enclosure, summary of articles in Ανεξαρτιτός. For example, while in Athens, Paschalis and Pavlides were viciously attacked in Ελληνική (Greek), 29 May 1932, by Kolokasides, see Papageorgiou, *Η Κυπριακή Ενωτική Κίνηση στην Αθήνα,*, 276.

[32] CO67/253/10, Palmer to Allen, 19 January 1934.

report of 1932'.³³ Regardless, the British authorities believed in a link with Greece from the beginning – namely that the assassination was ordered from Greece.

The newspaper articles sent to Cyprus by Waterlow reinforced this. Those published on 18, 19 and 23 January were editorials, probably influenced by the deported Cypriots, given the content, tone and phraseology of the attacks. These articles expressed no sympathy for Triantafyllides and focussed on the 'oppressive' British measures, which they claimed were unjustified because the crime was not political. On 18 January *Εστία* (Focus), a right-wing nationalist daily published by Achilles Kyrou (the brother of Alexis, the former consul in Cyprus, recalled because of his pro-*enosis* activities), was particularly scathing, claiming that the British rage directed against the nationalists (the five were interned on 13 January) was unparalleled and that they were using the 'mysterious assassination […] to create once more a savage terrorist situation'. It asserted that the measures were aimed at creating 'the impression that the murder […] is due to political motives' to stop new constitutional proposals.³⁴

> This intention is unjust, bad and cowardly. Unjust because the peaceable and patriotic Cypriot people can on no account be accused of using the weapon of political murder to satisfy its natural desires […].³⁵

Πατρίς (Country) published a letter on 24 January 1934 signed by 'A Cypriot', which seemingly convinced King that the motive was personal,³⁶ failing to read the article against the grain. The author had over a week after Triantafyllides's death to consider their words carefully. They attacked Triantafyllides as 'a traitor' and blamed his personal life and politics for his assassination. The title of the article asked rhetorically: 'Who is Triantafyllides who has been assassinated in Cyprus'? While arguing that 'personal vengeance, rather than anything else' was the motive, it answered its own question.

---

³³ CO67/253/10, secret, Palmer to Allen, 24 January 1934. This secret MI5 report could not be found.
³⁴ FO371/18391/860, Waterlow to Palmer, 27 January 1934, with translations from articles in *Πρωία*, 19 January 1934, *Έστια*, 18 January 1934 and *Ανεξαρτιτός*, 23 January 1934.
³⁵ Ibid, with translations from *Έστια*, 18 January 1934.
³⁶ FCO141/2497, King to Henniker-Heaton, 7 February 1934. Also, MSS Brit Emp s447, Blackall papers, *Πατρίς* article.

Antonios Triantafyllides who was assassinated in Cyprus was an extreme enemy of the struggle of Cypriots, he stood against the deeds of the Enosis endeavour of the people of Cyprus.

Until 1930 he had not mixed himself in politics openly, being content to undermine the struggle of his compatriots in a deceitful and satanical manner. He preferred to associate with the English in the Island, carefully avoiding connection with the Greeks, in order to gain the confidence of the English. He was a most able advocate, very diligent and on the other hand most revenging and an enemy of anything Hellenic.[37]

Was his use of 'assassination' and 'assassinated' (numerous times) a Freudian slip? In any event, 'A Cypriot' claimed that the British 'surrounded him with their friendship, and their special favouritism' and found 'in Triantafyllides an especially clever agent for their infernal objects'. He accused Triantafyllides of 'boasting that he is of an English conscience, and that on the occasion of the Administration of Cyprus passing into the hands of the Greeks, he would depart to England with his family'. The author further claimed that Triantafyllides had profited from the 1931 events, when 'he was rubbing his hands with pleasure' at the extra work and 'wildly speculated on these national cases', when 'other advocates were defending them free of charge'. He accused Triantafyllides of associating even more with the British during the 'persecutions, deportations, and imprisonments' after October 1931, when 'those very few Greek friends of the English stopped their connection with them fearing the rage of the persecuted people of Cyprus'. 'A Cypriot' claimed that Triantafyllides went further in 'advising and suggesting crushing measures rivalling his brother-in-law' Stelios Pavlides, who was also 'a traitor', as was Neoptolemos Paschalis. The letter criticised Triantafyllides for joining the advisory council, which was 'established to strangle the wish of Cyprus and to adulterate the national idea'. It went on to assert, 'Everyone realises that […] the private and public life of the victim, was bound to cause hate and vengeance on the part of the inhabitants' and that the 'Cypriots could quite well have cleared off all the traitors […] but they did not want to infect with assassinations, their struggle, which is so honest, gentle and beautiful'. Nevertheless, despite the author outlining the political motives that he would have to assassinate Triantafyllides, 'political motives should be excluded', and he believed that the British authorities would conclude that they 'acted

---

[37] Ibid., including *Πατρίς* (Country) article, 24 January 1934.

hurriedly' and would ultimately find that 'the motives of the assassination are personal reasons of revenge rather than political'.[38]

While the entire country mourned Triantafyllides's passing, 'A Cypriot' celebrated by launching a tirade against the victim, thus showing their motive to assassinate him. Undoubtedly, the author was one of the deported far right extremists, probably Loizides as the leading scribe, who used the word 'infernal' in attacks on those who had accepted government posts. The article had three aims: first to convince readers that this was not an assassination, but a murder for personal reasons; second, that the British had politicised the murder by blaming it on the right-wing nationalists to suppress the Cypriots; and third, that Cyprus was better off with Triantafyllides dead. The author could not hide his hatred of Triantafyllides, yet emphasised that those interned, his far right colleagues in Cyprus, were not responsible. The creation of a false personal motive to confuse investigators and the public was an obvious ploy of someone who may have been behind the assassination.[39]

Evidence linking the coterie in Athens and their friends in Cyprus to the assassination of Triantafyllides comes from Theophanis Theodotou, his father-in-law and a leading pro-*enosis* leader before his deportation in 1931. On 1 February 1934, Theodotou visited the Colonial Office uninvited and left two letters, dated 26 January and 30 January, while a third he sent direct to Palmer as instructed by the Colonial Office.[40] The Colonial Office told Palmer that they ordinarily would not allow a deported figure to visit the Colonial Office, but Theodotou had vital information on the assassination.[41] Theodotou had been an irresponsible hothead, but had never advocated organised violence against the authorities in pursuit of *enosis*.[42] In his first letter he declared: 'In my

---

[38] Ibid.
[39] This was not the only lack of sympathy for Triantafyllides. Galatopoulos, whom Triantafyllides represented in 1932 over his role in the violence in October 1931, although praising his brother-in-law, Panayiotis Cacoyiannis, for his contribution to Cyprus as a member of the executive council, had no sympathy for Triantafyllides in his 'memoirs' from 1937 after his release from prison. During his court case in 1932, Galatopoulos 'was looking with a rather suspicious eye on the late Triantafyllides, for he belonged to the so-called moderate type of politicians and to the group that had a good deal of intercourse with the Government circles'. This was although Triantafyllides had planned a defence, which Galatopoulos rejected. Galatopoulos, *From the Cruiser to the Jail Birds' Nest*, 108, 128–32.
[40] FCO141/2497, Cunliffe-Lister to Palmer, 1 February 1934; FCO141/2497, Theodotou to Palmer, 8 February 1934.
[41] CO67/253/11, Parkinson, CO, to Palmer, 1 February 1934.
[42] For a recent interpretation of his career until 1925, see Varnava, *British Cyprus and the Long Great War*, 40–41, 44–46, 51, 105, 109, 158–59, 165, 175–78, 185, 191–98, 205,

opinion the crime is political: and if no adequate measures are taken other assassinations might follow'. His wife's cousin, Mr Zachariades, a London-based merchant, had told him of threatening letters that Triantafyllides had received (one in November and another three days before the murder). Importantly, he revealed that on 23 January, Bishop Nicodemos, who was in London, had told him, as stated in the epigraph, that Loizides, Kolokasides and Tsangarides had invited Nicodemos to Athens to lead them to 'use all means, murders not excluded, against those Cypriots who co-operate with the Government'.[43] Theodotou tried to persuade them not to do it because it would work against Cyprus. This 'association' were the remnants of EREK now in Athens. This accorded with the initial view of the British authorities, which led them to intern the five nationalists with links to the deportees in Athens and the British belief that there was a connection with Athens.

The resort to violence by the four deportees in Athens was also confirmed by Ierotheos Kykkotis to Stavrinides. Because of their anger at an article in *Φωνή της Εκκλησίας* (Voice of the Church) on 24 February that there was widespread support in Cyprus for the immediate election of an archbishop at the exclusion of the two deported bishops, which was the view of Triantafyllides, the deportees in Athens, Kolokasides, Loizides and Tsangarides, visited the offices of *Φωνή της Εκκλησίας* to violently assault the editor, Mr Mavropoulos, who had called the police anticipating this reaction.[44] Meanwhile, the Cypriot authorities had intelligence in May 1934 that the deportees in Athens were stating openly 'to advocate methods of terrorism', and that the 'guiding spirits' were Makarios and Loizides.[45]

Not only had Theodotou implicated his fellow deportees in the assassination of Triantafyllides, but also suggested a way to prove it: '[…] if some *able* Cypriot was sent to Athens and became a member of the infernal association, he might find out more positive proof of the assassination […]'. He also suggested that the Cypriots be made to pay an indemnity to the Triantafyllides family so the government could show its support to those who sacrificed their lives in the service of the government and turn the people against those

---

210. For his career from 1925 until October 1931, see Georghallides, *Cyprus and the Governorship of Sir Ronald Storrs*, 76–77, 85, 94–98, 196–98, 201, 209, 378–80, 442–43, 474–75, 521, 564–65, 607, 611, 618, 634, 669, 692–94, 705.

[43] CO67/253/11, strictly confidential, Theodotou to Cunliffe-Lister, 26 January 1934, handwritten; FCO141/2497, strictly confidential, Theodotou to Cunliffe-Lister, 26 January 1934.

[44] FCO141/2483, secret, McLaughlan, postal censor, to CSC, 3 April 1934.

[45] FCO141/2464, summary of political situation, May-July 1934, 1 August 1934.

responsible to provide information.[46] In his next letter (30 January), Theodotou claimed that completed insurance forms were found in Triantafyllides's office, meaning that he feared assassination after receiving threatening letters. He accused the police of 'gross negligence of their duty' for not providing plain-clothed police protection. Theodotou also believed that the five interned men, who had all called Triantafyllides a traitor in Cypriot newspapers, should have been arrested as accomplices because now they could 'work for the non-discovery of the crime',[47] as 'A Cypriot' was trying to do. In his last letter, he claimed that the assassin may have come from Greece and returned there as a Greek boat had left Larnaca two hours after the shooting.[48] Palmer expressed his condolences, to which Theodotou thanked him,[49] but there was no further correspondence between them in the archives on the assassination.

As a political deportee, playing a more conciliatory role so he could return to Cyprus,[50] the British authorities questioned Theodotou's views, although they accorded with theirs, particularly Palmer's and Blackall's. The Deputy Police Commissioner, Jack Ashmore, told King that Theodotou should be told that a political motive was uncertain, claiming that Triantafyllides had 'immoral habits'. This statement comes after the newspapers from Athens had reached the Cypriot authorities, indicating that the police fell for the views of 'A Cypriot'. Also, the police possessed an insulting letter (dated 2 November), but it was not threatening according to Ashmore, contrary to Palmer's view. The police

---

[46] CO67/253/11, strictly confidential, Theodotou to Cunliffe-Lister, 26 January 1934, handwritten, not redacted; FCO141/2497, strictly confidential, Theodotou to Cunliffe-Lister, 26 January 1934.

[47] CO67/253/11, strictly confidential, Theodotou to Cunliffe-Lister, 26 January 1934, handwritten; FCO141/2497, strictly confidential, Theodotou to Cunliffe-Lister, 30 January 1934, typed.

[48] FCO141/2497, Theodotou to Palmer, 8 February 1934. He ended his letter stating that he believed that Triantafyllides had sacrificed his life for his country.

[49] FCO141/2497, Henniker-Heaton to Theodotou, 19 February 1934; FCO141/2497, Theodotou to Palmer, 4 March 1934.

[50] For Theodotou's efforts to return to Cyprus during the 1930s see: Rolandos Katsiaounis, 'Η Κυπριακή Παροικία του Λονδίνου και το Αρχιεπισκοπικό Ζήτημα της Κύπρου, 1928–1936' [The Cypriot Community of London and the Archiepiscopal Question of Cyprus, 1928–1936], *Annual of the Cyprus Research Centre* 22 (1996): 521–56; Evan Smith and Andrekos Varnava, 'Creating a "Suspect Community": Monitoring and Controlling the Cypriot Community in London and their Immigration to the UK', *English Historical Review* 132, no. 557 (2017): 1149–81. Theodotou returned to Cyprus in 1939 because of ill health. In 1936, in a petition asking for his return, his wife referred to the brutal assassination of Antonios. CO67/269/12, Styliani Theodotou to His Majesty, 4 February 1936.

stated that Triantafyllides had not asked for police protection and no life insurance application was found, while his life was already well insured.[51] This last point, particularly, brought into question Theodotou's letter, yet the issue of the threatening letter(s) to Triantafyllides, which Palmer acknowledged had been threatening, and other issues were dismissed, although they presented the possibility of a lead.

The threatening letters come up in both the colonial archive and newspapers. As discussed, *Φωνή της Κύπρου* claimed to have had evidence that Triantafyllides had received a letter three days before he was shot threatening his life if he did not resign from the advisory council.[52] Assassination was not only threatened on others, but it was even threatened to do to them what they had done to Triantafyllides. Six days after Triantafyllides had been shot, Michalakis Louisides, also on the advisory council, received an 'anonymous threatening letter', which stated: 'for the sake of your familiar (sic) you had better insure your life'.[53] Next day, another letter arrived: 'Resignation Death. Do you prefer life??? Three days' time'. The threat to kill him in three days echoed the threat claimed to have been made to Triantafyllides. On each side of the word 'resignation' there were two pots with flowers drawn with ink and on either side of the word 'death' two revolvers were drawn.[54] Louisides was panicked and wished to resign from the advisory council, but was convinced to stay by the police, who promised protection.[55] Equally important was the letter to Larnaca's municipal councillor, Michael Valdaserides, who was in his 70s, threatening to kill him 'like Triantafyllides', over his support for keeping the municipal market in its same location,[56] because it meant that someone had killed Triantafyllides for political reasons. To be sure, some of the threatening letters aimed at extortion, such as when Phylaktis Nikola Papa Phylakti was arrested for sending a letter threatening Eugenia Theodotou (a wealthy donor to social causes) with death like Triantafyllides unless she paid

---

[51] FCO141/2497, Ashmore to King, 20 February 1934. It is unlikely that the police had monitored Triantafyllides or had any evidence of his supposed 'immoral habits'.
[52] *Φωνή της Κύπρου*, 13 January 1934, 2. The Cypriot government knew about this claim. See FCO141/2497, anonymous to Henniker-Heaton, 13 January 1934.
[53] FCO141/2493, statement, Louisides, 19 January 1934 taken by I. M. Tilliro, LCCMP. The letter, which was sent from Famagusta, was signed 'F. E.'.
[54] FCO141/2493, statement, Louisides, 19 January 1934 taken by Tilliro. The letter, also sent from Famagusta, contained the handwritten letters LMII.
[55] FCO141/2493, pressing, secret & personal, Tilliro to LCCCID, Nicosia, 19 January 1934. This document was redacted. See also FCO141/2464, DCFam to Henniker-Heaton, 19 May 1934, in which it is stated that the authorities could not identify the author(s) of the letters to Louisides.
[56] *Ελευθερία*, 24 February 1934, 2.

him £40.⁵⁷ Then it was reported on 16 March that an anonymously signed letter to the Abbot of Mahairas Monastery, Mytrophanis, stated that Archimandrite Gregoris and Hieromonk Epiphanios had offered the man £100 to shoot him (the Abbot) like Triantafyllides, and advised him to take Holy Communion, unlike Triantafyllides who did not have time, because they would find someone else to do it. The police found a revolver and 27 bullets in Epiphanios's room, and the men were arrested.⁵⁸ And, finally in June, there was the threat to Nicholas Nicolaides, the Mayor of Paphos, written in modern Turkish, which stated that unless he stopped being tyrannical towards the poor he would find himself dead like Triantafyllides.⁵⁹ This last threat came after Dr Pigasiou had been released and hinted at being inspired by communism, yet the British never used this in forming their communist conspiracy theory regarding Triantafyllides's assassination.

Palmer had telegraphed Cunliffe-Lister on 17 January to say that several members of the advisory council had been threatened.⁶⁰ Two days later, he sent the 'threatening' letter dated 2 November to Cunliffe-Lister, referring to it as 'a threatening letter' (contradicting Ashmore), and claiming that its phraseology resembled that of an article signed by P. Stylianou (Polycarpos Stylianou Ioannides).⁶¹ The letter, dated a day after the newspapers had published Triantafyllides's reasons for joining the advisory council, referred to Triantafyllides as an 'infernal', the same word used by Loizides to describe the most wretched traitors and in the article by 'A Cypriot'; clearly the letter emanated from someone in EREK. The letter makes every insult possible against Triantafyllides, for example:

> You are buggers, pimps, procurers, cuckolds, vagabonds, murderers of the fatherland, sellers of the fatherland because had you not had these official qualifications you would have never accepted the appointment like another Judas Iscariot, like another Pausanias, like another nightmare against Nero and those surrounding him who are called – to our bad luck – Governors.⁶²

---

⁵⁷ *Πρωινή*, 3 March 1934, 4.
⁵⁸ *Χρόνος*, 16 March 1934, 4.
⁵⁹ *Πρωινή*, 13 June 1934, 4.
⁶⁰ CO67/253/10, telegram, Palmer to Cunliffe-Lister, 17 January 1934.
⁶¹ CO67/253/10, secret, Palmer to Cunliffe-Lister, 19 January 1934, enclosure, dossier on Papa Nicolaou and Polycarpos Ioannides. SA1/438/34, see dossiers on Markides and Polycarpos Ioannides, undated.
⁶² SA1/438/34, enclosing letter threatening Triantafyllides, 2 November 1933.

Clearly there is personal hatred, but it was inseparable from the political hatred, and they were willing to use violence. It even asked: 'When is that salutary hour to be when that magnanimous, superb giant Hitler will give us the signal "Now or Never"', thus divulging the author's Nazism. It then threatened to kill Triantafyllides in a group assault: 'Like lions we shall fall upon you'. As for a letter that Triantafyllides received days before being shot, none was found according to Palmer and the police, yet this does not mean that Triantafyllides had not received such a letter.[63]

Finally, Brewster Surridge, who had served the Cypriot government for decades and was the District Commissioner of Larnaca, reported the claim of a threatening letter to Triantafyllides and that the deportees in Athens were behind his assassination. While on leave in London, he sent the Colonial Office an extract from a letter he had received from a 'most prominent Greek newspaper reporter, a man who is in the know':

> The motive of the crime is political. He received a threatening letter asking him to resign from the advisory council otherwise death [...] I am of the firm opinion that the deported Bishop of Kyrenia and his camarilla of newspaper 'Protevousa' (the Capital) which he finances have their fingers in the crime. It is a pity to lose our best man. Our leading servant and a good patriot. A man who was not a demagogue of the "Zito I Enosis" (long live *enosis*) party.[64]

Surridge provided 'inside information' from this reporter, perhaps Wideson, who would have known Surridge, yet his information was also seemingly ignored.

Despite the evidence pointing to a conspiracy to assassinate Triantafyllides from the deportees in Athens and their associates in Cyprus, the British authorities decided that it was a communist conspiracy. Palmer informed the Colonial Office on 12 December 1934 that the police were 'practically certain of the identity of the man who shot Triantafyllides', describing him as a youth in gaol for attempting to kill one of the *muhtars* in Nicosia, which he was hired to do and the inference was that he was paid to shoot Triantafyllides too. Palmer stated that the motive of the communists was because Triantafyllides refused to defend them after the 1931 riots. Palmer opined that 'that may be one reason but I do not believe it was the only one' and

---

[63] Ibid.
[64] CO67/253/10, Surridge to Allen, 25 January 1934.

it leaves no doubt that it was not a crime of purely private and personal revenge, and thus that the action taken after it happened was pretty well justified, whatever the precise influence which prompted it was.[65]

To London, Palmer claimed that it was political and that it did not matter if it was from the far right or far left, vindicating his initial moves. But it did matter to Palmer. Blackall revealed in his diary for 15 December, two days after Palmer wrote to Cosmo Parkinson: 'Ashmore tells me that H. E. has told King (C.C.P.) that Triantafyllides's murderer had better not be prosecuted'. For Blackall this was 'an astounding thing and an interference with the administration of justice'; he would 'have no hand or part in it' and if there were evidence, he would advise 'in favour of a prosecution'.[66] It is unclear what he advised, although by not prosecuting the case (he was on sick leave during the court proceedings) one might believe that he had some misgivings. In his private papers he noted: 'although there were good grounds for suspecting who murdered Triantafyllides there was unfortunately insufficient evidence for a prosecution'.[67]

It also matters for this study, since the courts rejected the communist conspiracy theory. After being notified that charges would be laid against a young communist, the *Times* reported that Palmer would release those interned in connection with the assassination.[68] This was not entirely true: Dr Pigasiou and Pygmalion Ioannides had already been released on 2 June 1934.[69] Christodoulou was charged on 12 January.[70] King reported his acquittal to Palmer as 'the two judges who acquitted the accused were not prepared to accept the evidence of certain witnesses as being of the degree of reliability and trustworthiness called for in a trial for murder'. But the police still believed that Christodoulou and two prosecution witnesses were responsible. With no appeal against an acquittal possible according to Cypriot law, King asked Palmer to thank the police involved, which he did,[71] and Palmer informed Cunliffe-Lister.[72] Nobody questioned where it had gone wrong. Indeed, the *Cyprus Mail*, the only English

---

[65] CO67/253/10, confidential, Palmer to Parkinson, 12 December 1934.
[66] CVAR, ARF/00284, Blackall diary, 15 December 1934.
[67] MSS Brit Emp s447, Blackall papers, notes beneath *Πατρίς* article.
[68] *The Times*, 31 December 1934, 11.
[69] *Φωνή της Κύπρου*, 2 June 1934, 3.
[70] FCO141/2497, King to Henniker-Heaton, 11 January 1935.
[71] FCO141/2497, note, 27 February 1935; FCO141/2497, secret, Henniker-Heaton to King, 1 March 1935; FCO141/2497, secret, King to Henniker-Heaton, 1 March 1935.
[72] FCO141/2497, Palmer to Cunliffe-Lister, 4 March 1935.

language newspaper in the island at the time, insisted in April 1935 that Christodoulou was a communist and that 'luckily Communism has made little headway in Cyprus'.[73]

King's role in this case was mysterious. In his general police reports for 1934 and 1935, after describing the particulars of this 'outstanding' case, he disclosed that

> After lengthy and exceedingly difficult investigations, coupled with most commendable perseverance and patience, the Police, in the first weeks of 1935 began proceedings against an accused. One of the greatest obstacles to the investigations was the fact that the motive for the crime was very obscure, and the deceased was unable to assist in this respect before he died. It is a striking example of the inherent reluctance of the Cypriot to assist the police, that in spite of a reward of £1,000 being offered for evidence or information leading to a conviction, not a single person came forward voluntarily with trustworthy and reliable evidence.[74]

This was indeed unusual, since in the court it was revealed that three witnesses came forward as soon as Christodoulou was arrested for the attempted murder of Anastasides to reveal that he had admitted to the shooting of Triantafyllides and that Dr Pigasiou had paid him. Then in his 1935 report, King revealed that the 'trial of the accused for the murder of Antonios Triantafyllides [...] ended in acquittal by a majority verdict of the Assize Court at Nicosia'.[75] If the British pursued the case legitimately, his performance must be questioned. This would explain his accepting a transfer to a lesser role and pay as Deputy Commissioner of Police in Nigeria in March 1937. If he participated in a cover-up, the transfer ensured that it remained covered up.[76]

The switch from a nationalist to a communist plot is easily understood within the context of the obsession of the Cypriot authorities to suppress communism and their failure to read the evidence on Triantafyllides's assassination

---

[73] *Cyprus Mail*, 17 April 1935, 2. See also *Πρωινή*, 27 February 1935, 1, which claimed that the case had shown that the government needed to take measures to develop the working class away from a life of crime.

[74] *Cyprus: Report on the Cyprus Police Force for the Year 1934*, by W. C. C. King, CGPO, Nicosia, 1935, 13.

[75] *Cyprus: Report on the Cyprus Police Force for the Year 1935*, by W. C. C. King, CGPO, Nicosia, 1936, 18.

[76] *Cyprus: Report on the Cyprus Police Force for the Year 1937*, by W. S. Gulloch, CGPO, Nicosia, 1938, 3.

against the grain. Soon after August 1926, when the communists formed the CPC, the British authorities suppressed it, deporting two of its leaders.[77] This continued, especially after October 1931, when numerous communists were deported and others placed under house arrest in isolated parts of the island, laws were passed to facilitate their prosecution and the CPC was banned in 1933.[78] The authorities were always more wary of communism than nationalism (and fascism) in Cyprus, epitomised by Palmer's view to the Colonial Office, only days before Triantafyllides was assassinated: 'At present the Church with all its corruption is anti-Communist, and that is a big asset'.[79] Six months later, after Dr Pigasiou and Pygmalion Ioannides had been released, Palmer opined to Cunliffe-Lister that the Athens fanatics had moderated their tone against the Cypriot government and in Cyprus there were

> distinct indications of a wish on the part of all but a few extremists to improve relations with Government [...] [and] "Enosis" is, I have a strong reason to think [...] waning as a formula for expressing this dissatisfaction (from 1931).[80]

Palmer claimed that the threat from far right extremists in Cyprus had waned, yet this is because they went quiet to divert attention from the evidence against them. Perhaps this is why nobody, in writing at least, queried the testimony that Pigasiou paid Christodoulou to assassinate Triantafyllides. There was no effort to connect Loizides with Pigasiou and Polycarpos Ioannides, or Loizides with Christodoulou (both were from Kato Dikomo). Put simply, Christodoulou had claimed that Mathaiou had shot Triantafyllides as part of a communist conspiracy and other witnesses had stated that Christodoulou had been a communist, so it must have been the communists behind it. This neatly fitted the Cypriot government's anti-communist obsession. It even allowed them to ignore information, discussed earlier, from Waterlow in Athens in May and June 1934, that Loizides, Makarios, Tsangarides and Kolokasides had created the *Society of Friends of Cyprus* at the start of 1934, to use terrorism to achieve *enosis*, in opposition to the former Greek consul in Cyprus, Alexis Kyrou, who supported greater patience.[81] It was not the communists who were openly advocating terrorism and assassination, but the right-wing extremists.

---

[77] See FCO141/2404.
[78] See the heavily redacted file, FCO141/2455.
[79] CO67/254/4, secret, Palmer to Parkinson, 10 January 1934.
[80] CO67/254/3, secret, Palmer to Cunliffe-Lister, 22 June 1934.
[81] CO67/255/2, secret, Palmer to Cunliffe-Lister, 19 June 1934, including enclosures.

But is this a satisfactory explanation for the British communist conspiracy theory which was rejected in court? Their failure was startling, since they knew soon after Christodoulou was arrested for the attempted murder of Anastasiades and during the pre-hearing that their own witnesses contradicted it and implicated Dr Pigasiou, whom they had suspected from the start. Did the British authorities attempt to cover up the evidence of a far right conspiracy? There is no concrete evidence for this, but there were a series of suspicious behaviours.

It is highly suspicious that the British authorities did not pursue the evidence, including from their witnesses, that implicated Pigasiou. On 7 May 1934, King had advised the release of Pygmalion Ioannides and Pigasiou, which Palmer approved on 26 May and occurred on 2 June.[82] Pygmalion Ioannides was arrested because his club (*Ελευθερία*/Freedom) gathered both the right- and left-wing anti-colonial lower and middle classes. He was not a member of EREK, although associated with Papa Nicolaou.[83] His highest political office was as a councillor for the Nicosia Municipality from 1946 to 1949, under Ioannis Clerides, who had won the mayorship of Nicosia from Dervis with the support of AKEL as a centre-left-wing candidate.[84] On the other hand, Pigasiou was a prime suspect. His release so early, while Papa Nicolaou and Markides remained interned until 21 December 1934, when Christodoulou was about to be charged,[85] and when Polycarpos Ioannides remained interned until November 1935, is mysterious.[86] Why was Pigasiou released? Papa Nicolaou and Markides were released upon agreeing not to involve themselves in seditious politics, and Papa Nicolaou moved to Athens until 1946, when he returned to Cyprus after Makarios and the other exiles were also permitted to return.[87] It is unknown under what conditions Pigasiou and Pygmalion Ioannides were released, but they were released with other nationalists and communists.[88] This did not draw suspicion on the release of Pigasiou, which is an important point if he had agreed to work as a British

---

[82] SA1/438/34, King to Henniker-Heaton, 7 May 1934; Henniker-Heaton to King, 26 May 1934; *Φωνή της Κύπρου*, 2 June 1934, 3.
[83] CO67/253/10, secret, Palmer to Cunliffe-Lister, 19 January 1934, enclosure, dossier on Pygmalion Ioannides.
[84] Katsiaounis, *Η Διασκεπτική*, 147, 350.
[85] SA1/438/34, Hart-Davis to Henniker-Heaton, 2 January 1935; *The Times*, 31 December 1934, 11.
[86] SA1/461/34, correspondence between Ioannides and the government over his requests to be released.
[87] SA1/438/34, Hart-Davis to Henniker-Heaton, 2 January 1935; Coudounaris, *Βιογραφικόν Λεξικόν Κυπρίων*, 285.
[88] SA1/438/34, Lists of those interned; King to Henniker-Heaton, 7 May 1934.

informer. Also suspicious was the British police stating in December 1934 (a week before Papa Nicolaou and Markides were released) that Polycarpos Ioannides was 'unrepentant and fanatical', implying that the other four were repentant about something.[89] Then there was the sudden death of Pigasiou aged 54 in August 1939, for which no cause was reported and little fanfare made in the newspapers, beyond mentioning his contribution in the Balkan Wars. Curiously, Miltiades Coureas gave the eulogy.[90]

Finally, there was Blackall's evidence that Palmer did not want to prosecute Christodoulou.[91] One reason for this hesitation could be that the prosecution's communist conspiracy case could not convict Christodoulou when the prosecution witnesses risked implicating Pigasiou and the far right conspiracy that Palmer now wanted covered up. Blackall knew Palmer well, serving under him in the Northern Provinces of Nigeria. He described Palmer as 'an autocratic individual', who was 'disposed to treat the Cypriots as if they were primitive Nigerian natives'. Displeased when Palmer was appointed to Cyprus, Blackall claimed that Palmer had no use for the advisory council, fitting his autocratic nature and his concerns to ensure there was no repeat assassination on his watch.[92] He seemed to believe that there would be no more assassinations from about six months after the assassination of Triantafyllides, and perhaps he had 'a deal' with the far right, or some of them (i.e., Pigasiou), to protect them from prosecution in exchange for no more, and to cover up what they seemingly did to Triantafyllides, while also trying to drive another nail in the coffin of the communists. Meanwhile, Palmer also kept referring to there being a 'personal side' behind the assassination. William Battershill, who replaced Henniker-Heaton in early 1935 and Palmer in 1939, disclosed that Palmer excluded him from decision-making. He also revealed that Palmer's main adviser was James Drogo Montagu, who had replaced Hart-Davis in January 1935, and who Dervis had 'in his pocket', since they were both cabaret fans and Dervis, 'a great womaniser', had even organised to take Palmer to the cabaret. Battershill found some of the stories about Palmer's actions in Cyprus to be 'very odd and disturbing', but said no more.[93] Could this remark have been related to the assassination of

---

[89] SA1/438/34, Minute on Polycarpos Ioannides, 15 December 1934.
[90] *Φωνή της Κύπρου*, 26 August 1939, 2; *Κυπριακός Φύλαξ*, 27 August 1939, 2; *Ελευθερία*, 29 August 1939, 3.
[91] CVAR, ARF/00284, Blackall diary, 15 December 1934.
[92] MSS Brit Emp s447, Blackall papers, notes beneath, Blackall to Allen, 4 July 1935, also notes beneath, secret, Blackall to Colonial Secretary, on constitution of advisory council, 20 November 1935.
[93] MSS Brit Emp s467, papers of Sir William Denis Battershill, 18 June 1936, Bodleian Library, Special Collections, University of Oxford.

Triantafyllides? It is unlikely that those behind the assassination had a personal motive that connected with Palmer, since he was hardly in the island before Triantafyllides was assassinated. But during the course of 1934, the far right may have obtained something more personal against someone in the colonial administration, including Palmer, which risked coming out in court, which led Palmer to cover up the far right's seeming assassination of Triantafyllides.

Then what of the role of Paschalis? Was he merely an instrument of British actions, or did he have his own motivations? Paschalis, as a close associate and friend of Triantafyllides, must have wanted a conviction for his friend and his family. His initial views on who was behind the assassination were clear and he advised the internment of the five. Yet Paschalis, being an anti-communist, would have accepted pushing the communist conspiracy theory. But more so he would have feared that the most likely perpetrators, the right-wing extremists, had him in their sights, given their vitriol against him. Did this fear play a part in him pursuing the failed communist conspiracy theory? If so, the entire proceedings were aimed at drawing attention away from the initial impulse to blame the right-wing extremists in a cover-up. By doing this, Paschalis was protecting himself, the government, those Cypriots appointed to government and state positions, and to the executive and advisory councils.

This makes some sense if those responsible had stopped their assassinations, as they seemingly did after making threats to various others, fearing being discovered, satisfied that they had placed considerable fear in the community and that they had eliminated the most intelligent, astute, charismatic, and popular of those politicians who may have forged a path to self-government. The executive and advisory councils continued to function, and although there was cooperation and demands from various Cypriots, such as Ioannides Clerides and George Vassiliades, who replaced Triantafyllides, for a new constitution, the assassination of Triantafyllides had caused doubt for the authorities, especially Palmer, who had authoritarian instincts anyway. Therefore, the far right had succeeded in stopping an interim constitutional process and it meant much to them to not be found out, because, as was said in the letter probably penned by Loizides, they did not want to poison the *enosis* demand with assassinations, or rather, they did not want to be found to have done so. And this aspect, the remembering and especially the forgetting of the Triantafyllides case is especially important in understanding who was probably responsible, and why his assassination is significantly connected to historical events in Cyprus since.

Chapter 4

THE ASSASSINATION OF TRIANTAFYLLIDES AND THE EOKA CONNECTION

> One very important point which should not be forgotten is that a very large number of sound-minded Greeks (i.e. Greek Cypriots), not belonging to any of the two parties (AKEL or KEK), find it extremely difficult to speak publicly and express their views openly on this subject (*enosis*), for the simple reason that they would be running the risk of being accused as traitors by the others who appear to be the real enemies of this country.
>
> Anonymous Greek Cypriot to Sir Cosmo Parkinson,
> 1 September 1944.

You may think there is nobody alive to recall the assassination of Antonios Triantafyllides. Well you would be wrong. Antonis Pitrakkou, a grand old man and my wife's uncle by marriage, remembers it well. Uncle Antonis is a great storyteller. One day I was telling him about my research on the assassination of Triantafyllides. At length he stopped me and asked: 'Although I'm from Rizokarpasso, you know I was born in Aglanja?' I said: 'yes I know'. He then leaned forward and recounted:

> I remember the assassination of Antonakis Triantafyllides well. I was about eight and it was not long after that we moved to my parent's village of Rizokarpasso. I remember my father coming home in the evening (13 January) and saying sadly: "they've killed Triantafyllides, our best one". Even as young as 8, I understood and sensed the sadness and shock. How could I forget.[1]

We were both astonished and it is amazing that a migrant to Adelaide, Australia, in 1948, and now 94, could recall, yet, as he said: 'how could

---

[1] Author interview with Antonis Pitrakkou, 13 February 2020.

I forget'. The fear and shock in the Greek Cypriot community were palpable. And the comment 'our best one', shows that uncle Antonis's father, an ordinary worker, considered Triantafyllides the best politician going around.

The way the past is remembered and forgotten are integral to forming state-controlled national histories and identities.[2] The degree of state control depends on the character of the state and the level of nation-building that elites perceive is necessary. The control is greatest in postcolonial societies that maintain the rage against the colonial authority and in divided societies – Cyprus is both.[3] I have previously shown how one of the largest enlistments in the British forces during the Great War, the Cypriot Mule Corps, was silenced from Cypriot historical consciousness and historiography.[4] What is remembered are events twisted by nationalist revisionism to fit the script of the Greek or Turkish nations in Cyprus, while events that cannot be twisted, particularly those that show the integration of Cypriot communities, are silenced or distorted.[5] The assassination of Triantafyllides is connected to this nationalist revisionism, since his story became a victim to this silence and manipulation. But his assassination was distorted well before Cyprus became a postcolonial state and dates to immediately after the deed, with the British possibly contributing to it with their botched prosecution or cover-up. Not only did the likely perpetrators try to cover up their deed, but were conscious of building a far right nationalist narrative. They could only do that by avoiding blame and silencing or dismissing the event and other narratives of cooperation with the British authorities.

---

[2] For example, Anderson, *Imagined Communities*.

[3] Papadakis, 'The Politics of Memory'; Papadakis, 'Greek Cypriot Narratives'; Philippou and Varnava, 'Constructions of Solution(s) to the Cyprus Problem'.

[4] Varnava, 'The Politics of Forgetting' ', 291–303; Varnava, *Serving the Empire in the Great War*, 210–26.

[5] For example, the Ethnarchic role of Archbishop Sophronios, see Andrekos Varnava, 'Sophronios III, 1865–1900: The Last of the "Old" and the First of the "New" Archbishop-*Ethnarchs*?', in Varnava and Michael, *The Archbishops of Cyprus in the Modern Age*, 106–47. Then there were a series of books/pamphlets in the 1950s from Greece, aimed at proving the Greekness of the Cypriots as they embarked upon their violent struggle for *enosis*, aimed at a Western and Greek readership, contradicting the view that *enosis* was popular in Greece and Cyprus. Tassos G. Lekka, *Κύπρος: Η Κατεχόμενη Ελλάς* [Cyprus: The Occupied Hellas] (Dialismas, Athens, 1952); Nicholas Kl. Lanitis (who had been deported in 1931), *Η Δούλη Ελλάς του Νότου* [The Slaves of Hellas of the South] (Athens, 1954); Sergios A. Gialistras, *Hellas and Cyprus* (trans.) G. A. Trypanis (Athens, 1955); N. G. Photias, *The Island of Cyprus* (Athens: Rotary Club of Athinai,1956); Zenon G. Rossides, *The Problem of Cyprus* (Athens, 1957); *Cyprus: Touchstone for Democracy* (Athens: Union of Journalists of the Athens Newspapers, 1958).

Particularly telling was the choice of silence and distortion. When prompted about the assassination, the response would refer to the personal motive theory, keeping alive the rumours, ensuring that Triantafyllides was portrayed in an unsavoury light, both as regards his personal life and politics, and responsible for his own assassination. Silence and distortion were adopted by necessity as the blame followed the far right nationalists as soon as Triantafyllides died. The personal motive theory was chosen over blaming their rivals, the communists, whom the British accused of the crime. It would have been easy for the far right to blame the communists, who were weak after being suppressed by the British, but they preferred to blame the dead Triantafyllides. Switching from the personal motive theory that they had created after the assassination to blaming the communists risked opening questions on the political motive that they would prefer to avoid. Thus, the far right have avoided scrutiny, until now.

Also significant is that the communists have never accused the far right of the assassination. By 1935, the communists were thoroughly suppressed, functioning underground, and too weak to fight the accusations that they ordered the assassination, or to accuse the far right of it. Equally important is the formation of AKEL in April 1941. AKEL considered itself the successor of the CPC, yet its relationship with the CPC has never been comfortable because the CPC opposed *enosis* in favour of an anti-colonial movement of Greek and Turkish Cypriots to create an independent state.[6] There was no need to address the accusations against the CPC over the assassination, so there was no reason to address who was behind it. The explanation cannot be complete without understanding that postcolonial Cyprus was dominated by ex-EOKA cadres and intellectuals, which AKEL accepted.

What emerged in the postcolonial Republic of Cyprus after the violence unleashed by EOKA in April 1955, reciprocated by the colonial state, and countered by TMT, was the '*Eokatisation*' of the Greek Cypriot community, as the state was dominated by former EOKA cadres (and in the Turkish Cypriot case, by TMT). One could, therefore, call post-colonial Cyprus the '*Eokatokratia*' (held by EOKA, as opposed to '*Turkokratia*', Turkish held, and '*Bretanokratia*', British held). The EOKA and TMT-led government enshrined the worship of EOKA and TMT within both communities, while leading their communities into a Civil War in 1963–64 (ironically, EOKA had splintered into several paramilitary groups by then), and the first partition of the island, with Turkish Cypriots moving into enclaves.[7] This further enshrined their

---

[6] Katsourides, *The History of the Communist Party in Cyprus*, 173–95.
[7] See Stephen Xydis, *Cyprus: Reluctant Republic* (The Hague: Mouton, 1974); Alan James, *Keeping the Peace in the Cyprus Crisis of 1963–1964* (New York: Palgrave, 2001); Makarios Drousiotis, *The First Partition: Cyprus 1963–1964* (Nicosa: Alfadi, 2008).

oppositional nationalisms and silenced any Cypriotism.[8] A decade later the complete geographical separation of the two communities occurred after the Greek Junta's coup against President Makarios III and the Turkish military intervention. Despite AKEL supporting the presidential election of the independent George Vassiliou in 1988 and having their party leader, Demetris Christofias, elected in 2008, the '*Eokatokratia*' has never really been challenged. AKEL has been complicit, particularly in supporting Makarios for president (from the mid-1960s) and after his death former EOKA figures Spyros Kyprianou (1977–88) and Tassos Papadopoulos (2003–8). Thus, the silence and distortion around the assassination of Triantafyllides suited the far right that was likely responsible, and the far left who was accused of being responsible, because Triantafyllides did not fit their narratives of national liberation, making the cover-up easier.

The link between those likely to have organised the assassination, with two other assassinations and the founding of EOKA, indicates their predisposition for political violence. Triantafyllides may not be the first assassination in the name of *enosis*, with the mysterious murder of Dr Angelos Zemenides in January 1933 in London. Zemenides was an anti-communist Anglophile, who started the Cypriot Brotherhood of St Barnabas in London with the support of the British authorities. The aim was to steer Cypriots away from communism, which was popular amongst them in London, and pro-*enosis* nationalism, which was not popular with them there, but could develop. Zemenides made enemies from both the far right and far left for his pro-British views, anti-communism and efforts to develop the English-speaking of Cypriots and their identity as Cypriots. Although there is no evidence to connect the deported fanatics to his death, they had opportunity and motive, and the case resembles the assassination of Triantafyllides. Zemenides was shot at his home and the investigation shifted from a suspected assassination to personal motive, as Theodosios Petrou was acquitted of murdering Zemenides over money.[9] Despite opposition from the Venizelos government, by January 1933, Loizides (January 1932), Tsangarides (March), Kolokasides (May), and Makarios (December) settled in Athens,[10] so they had time to organise the killing of Zemenides, which they could have done from Athens anyway.

---

[8] For an anthropological approach see, Papadakis, 'The Politics of Memory and of Forgetting in Cyprus'; Papadakis, 'Greek Cypriot Narratives of History and Collective Identity'.

[9] Smith and Varnava, 'Creating a "Suspect Community"'.

[10] Loizides, *Ατυχη Κύπρος*, 44–45; Tsangarides, *Το Ημερολόγιου ενος Εξόριστου*, 72–73; Georghallides, 'The Cyprus Revolt', 96–112.

The link between the possible assassins of Zemenides and the probable assassins of Triantafyllides was made by Pyrros Giannopoulou Ipeirotou, a Greek journalist and author. In his 1956 self-published book, Ipeirotou made the extraordinary claim that Zemenides and Triantafyllides were assassinated because of their close relations with the British. Although he called the assassination of Triantafyllides 'that mysterious murder', the motives were political, 'based on the outcry which the Greek people of the island had against the victim, due to his willingness to serve the foreign occupiers of Cyprus'. Not only was this the line peddled by the Cypriot fanatics in Athens, but Ipeirotou also agreed with their attacks on Triantafyllides and the British, particularly for interning the five pro-*enosis* extremists.[11]

So why did Ipeirotou link the two assassinations? Ipeirotou was first a socialist, an ardent anti-Venizelist, staunch Royalist, and then a supporter of Ioannis Metaxas, and finally a fascist, anti-Semite. His books today are rare finds and betray his support for Royalism, namely King Constantine and Ioannis Metaxas, a Germanophile military figure and dictator of Greece (1935–41). As his books indicate, he was anti-Albanian, anti-Italian, anti-Bulgarian, anti-Turk, anti-Soviet as they were, in his eyes, the enemies of Greece, so it is unsurprising that he was anti-British when it came to Cyprus.[12] Ipeirotou had contacted Storrs in November 1931 about visiting Cyprus to report on the October 1931 riots: Storrs ignored him.[13] His books on Cyprus are pro-*enosis* propaganda and reveal his close relationship with Makarios. Why in 1956 would he reveal that Zemenides and Triantafyllides were assassinated for the same reasons? His books were summaries of the views of the deported Cypriots in Athens. Had they confessed? And in the spirit of 1956, during the peak of the EOKA period, with Makarios dead, was he showing off that EOKA had a lineage?

---

[11] Pyrros Giannopoulos Ipeirotou, *Η Μάχη της Κύπρου, 1878–1956* [The Battle of Cyprus, 1878–1956] (Athens: P. G. Ipeirotou, 1956), , 46–47.

[12] Pyrros Giannopoulos Ipeirotou, *Αι εκλογαί της 6 Δεκεμβρίου 1915: Πολιτικός λόγος* [The Elections of 6 December 1915: Political Reason] (Athens, 1916); Pyrros Giannopoulos Ipeirotou, *Οι Ιταλοί εν Ηπείρω* [*The Italians in Ipeiros*] (Athens, 1917); Pyrros Giannopoulos Ipeirotou, *Η Στάσις του Ιω. Μεταξά και ο Θρίαμβος της Επαναστάσεως του 1922* [The Stand of Ion. Metaxas and the triumph of the 1922 Revolution] (Athens, 1923); Pyrros Giannopoulos Ipeirotou, *Ο Κωνσταντινισμός και ο Μεταξάς* [Constantinism and Metaxas] (Athens, 1926); Pyrros Giannopoulos Ipeirotou, *Η Ρωσσία Καταρρευουσα: Η Ελλας Φραγμός εις την Σλαβικήν Επέκτασην* [The Russian Trajectory: Hellas as the Barrier to Slavic Expansion] (Athens, 1949). I purchased *Η Μάχη της Κύπρου, 1878–1956* years ago.

[13] Papageorgiou, *Η Κυπριακή Ενωτική Κίνηση στην Αθήνα*, 373.

By 1956, EOKA terrorism, British state terrorism and Turkish Cypriot terrorism had made the island into a dangerous place. While Greek Cypriots are indoctrinated about the 'heroic' EOKA struggle, historians have also been preoccupied with it. This predates the start of its operations on 1 April 1955, back to the decision to form EOKA in Athens in 1951. For this reason, there is much knowledge on those responsible for forming EOKA and their roles in it.[14] Also, the hero worship has allowed for EOKA cadres and their supporters (such as Charles Foley, the sympathetic editor of the *Times of Cyprus* during the emergency period) to inadvertently write freely about their roles and exploits, with some embellishment.[15]

In preparing society to use violence, the far right needed to convert the peasantry and labouring classes into *enosis* faithful and the youth into violent tools against the British and those opposed to EOKA.[16] After much planning since 1951,[17] violence started in April 1955. The violence involved using archetypical terrorist methods, namely, both urban and rural guerrilla warfare, including sabotage, and targeted bombings and assassinations.[18] These assassinations were primarily against those opposed to EOKA methods, or who worked for the administration, reminiscent of EREK's threats in the 1930s.

EREK members still alive, including those deported and living in Athens, remained prominent members of Cypriot society. They were to the right of the Cypriot Nationalist Party (KEK) formed in June 1943 and led from January 1944 by the Mayor of Nicosia, Dervis. KEK aimed to unite all the anti-communist and pro-*enosis* right-wing nationalists, whether fanatical or moderate. Although Dervis had been elected Mayor in 1929, from December 1931 all mayors were British appointed, and being, at that time, a loyalist, had no trouble being appointed, and developed very close relations with Palmer. But his power waned under Battershill and with the rise of communism, he

---

[14] Crawshaw, *The Cyprus Revolt*; Holland, *Britain and the Revolt in Cyprus*; Ioannides Stefanidis, *Isle of Discord: Nationalism, Imperialism and the Making of the Cyprus Problem* (NewYork: New York University Press, 1999); French, *Fighting EOKA*. The best is the last by French.

[15] Foley, *Island in Revolt*; George Grivas, *The Memoirs of General Grivas*, ed. Charles Foley (London: Longmans1964); Charles Foley, *Legacy of Strife: Cyprus from Rebellion to Civil War* (Harmondsworth: Penguin, 1964); Elenitsa Seraphim-Loizou, *The Cyprus Liberation Struggle, 1955–1959: Through the Eyes of a Woman EOKA Area Commander*, trans. John Vickers (Nicosia: Epiphaniou, 2000) (Greek, 1982); Andreas Azinas, *50 Years of Silence: Cyprus' Struggle for Freedom: My EOKA Secret File* (Nicosia: Airwaves, 2002).

[16] Grivas, *Memoirs of General Grivas*, 28–34; Crawshaw, *The Cyprus Revolt*, 175, 244–55, 190, 257, 280–2, 315–17, 406; French, *Fighting EOKA*, 89–90, 110–11, 159–70, 281, 294–95.

[17] Grivas, *Memoirs of General Grivas*, 13–32.

[18] George Grivas, *Guerrilla Warfare and EOKA's Struggle*, trans. A. A. Pallis (London: Longmans, 1964), 91–95, 101–6.

felt threatened. The Greek consul in Cyprus reported in 1945 and 1948 that KEK served the material interests of 'a certain social class', had no national appeal and was driven more by fear of communism than a desire for *enosis*.[19] After British troops entered Athens on 13 October 1944, Dervis, tried to capitalise on what appeared was a new chapter in Anglo-Hellenic relations, convincing his Greek and Turkish Cypriot councillors to request the return of Bishop Makarios and the other deportees.[20] The government was initially opposed, as was the Secretary of State.[21] Thereafter, the Cypriot press began a campaign to deceive the authorities and the Cypriot people into believing that Makarios was in such poor health that he should return to live out his last years, that he had been a victim of the Nazi occupation and had supported the communist resistance.[22] This last suggestion was too much for Polycarpos Ioannides, who poured cold water on it.[23] As for his ill health, those who visited Makarios in January 1945 at a sanitorium at Voula reported on his 'good health'.[24] Unsurprisingly, Makarios's fascist friend, Ipeirotou, claimed that he and other Cypriots in Athens had not collaborated with the Nazis or collaborationist regime, preferring instead to suffer in poverty and illness, and that they even helped the British with food.[25]

The evidence, however, reveals that Makarios and his friends were Nazi collaborators. British intelligence knew from January 1940 that Loizides was notorious for 'working as a German agent in Athens [...] [and] in July 1940 he was expelled to the Greek Islands by the Greek authorities', well before Greece entered the war.[26] His activities from 1942 to 1944 are uncertain, but he worked in the German set-up courts. There were numerous far right, including fascist, groups before the Axis occupation, while others appeared soon after the occupation. Numerous Cypriots belonged to these collaborationist groups, including the paramilitary units, and others still in the Waffen-SS Poulos Verband, while Achilles and Alexis Kyrou, who were less extreme than Loizides in the 1930s over Cyprus, were members of the newly formed 'Organisation of Pioneers of the New Europe'.[27] UK and US intelligence

---

[19] Alecou, *Communism and Nationalism in Postwar Cyprus*, 15, 18, 31–38.
[20] FCO141/2617, Dervis to DCNic, 19 October 1944.
[21] FCO141/2617, AGoC to CO, 23 October 1944; FCO141/2617, SSC to AGoC, 27 October 1944.
[22] FCO141/2617, translation, *Κυπριακός Τύπος*, 9 December 1944.
[23] FCO141/2617, Ioannides to Stavrinides (*Ελευθερία*), 14 January 1945.
[24] FCO141/2617, postcard, C. A. S. Papadopoulos to Dervis, 23 January 1945.
[25] Ipeirotou, *Η Μάχη της Κύπρου*, 53.
[26] FCO141/4281, top secret, KEK Dossier, 1949, see Loizides entry in index.
[27] Markos Vallianatos, *The Untold History of Greek Collaboration with Nazi Germany (1941–1944)* (Athens: Pelekys Books, 2014), 182, 190, 196.

believed that Loizides was a collaborator, either for the regime (or one of the affiliated fascist groups), its notorious Security Battalions, or 'Organisation X', formed by Colonel George Grivas, a Greek Cypriot by birth, in 1941 after the Axis occupation. After the war, 'X' claimed that it fought the Nazis, but its main aim was to stop a communist takeover after the war, offering to collaborate with the Nazis against the resistance, which was initially rejected. Bishop Makarios financially supported 'X'. Loizides probably joined it in August 1943, when all the organisations of the collaborationist regime did. In October 1943, the British brought the militant far right organisations, including 'X', together to prevent communist control after liberation, and 'X' played a vital role in the British anti-communist action from October 1944.[28] In November and December 1944, the Cypriot government was informed by many of the 300 Cypriot POWs, who had escaped from Italy, that they had been captured in Greece, betrayed by Makarios.[29] Yet in January 1945 Loizides appealed to return to Cyprus erroneously claiming that he had 'refrained from every political movement' while in Athens, had opposed fascism since 1935 and had rejected Nazi overtures to speak out against the British.[30] Makarios joined him in February, because now 'Anglo-Hellenic interests coincide and must continue to coincide for the future'.[31] When Greece was aligned with Britain during the war, Anglo-Hellenic interests had not aligned, but now they had because the enemy was communism.

This was the key factor in Charles Woolley, the Governor since October 1941, changing his position. On 27 February 1945 the executive council, which rarely made such important decisions, recommended the return of the deportees. It was acknowledged that Makarios had openly supported

---

[28] Ibid; Loizides, *Άτυχη Κύπρος*, 7–8; Christopher M. Woodhouse, *Apple of Discord: A Survey of Recent Greek Politics in Their International Setting* (London: Hutchinson, 1948), 31; Mark Mazower, *Inside Hitler's Greece: The Experience of Occupation, 1941–44* (New Haven: Yale University Press, 1993), 378; David Close, *The Origins of the Greek Civil War* (London: Longman, 1995), 114–15; Stefanidis, *Isle of Discord*, 249; Dimitris Kousouris, *Δίκες τών Δοσίλογων 1944–1949* (Trials of Collaborationists 1944–1949) (Athens: Polis, 2015), 82, 100–1, 115, 459–60; Alecou, *Communism and Nationalism in Postwar Cyprus*, 78–84.

[29] FCO141/2617, letter to Acheson, 21 November 1944; extract from redacted letter, 18 December 1944; FCO141/2874, report on interviews to Megaw, 18 November 1944. The British believed that they were communists, but this does not invalidate their evidence. They travelled across Cyprus chanting 'down with *enosis*' and told Woolley that they did not want *enosis*. Ibid., Foot to CO, 21 November 1944; CCPC to CSC, 2 December 1944.

[30] FCO141/2677, Loizides to Woolley, 17 January 1945.

[31] FCO141/2677, Makarios to Woolley, 6 February 1945.

the Metaxas dictatorship, had probably been a Nazi collaborator, but would also strongly oppose AKEL and Leontios's efforts to unite the Left and Right behind *enosis*. It was also stated that there was a greater chance of violence emanating from AKEL, while Hugh Foot, the Colonial Secretary, believed that the time had come to allow Makarios to return.[32] Woolley told Oliver Stanley, the Secretary of State for the Colonies, on 31 March 1945 that he had reversed his decision of October 1944 and now supported the return of the deportees and revoking the Church Laws of 1937 prohibiting the election of a deported bishop or one found guilty of sedition, based on 'the most important of all the new developments of recent years [...] the rise of the AKEL party'. Whether a Nazi collaborator or not, Makarios opposed Leontios and his 'unholy alliance' with AKEL and

> [...] every possible step must be taken by strengthening the Church and its backing of conservative nationalists and villagers to counter the increasingly dangerous influence of the AKEL party.[33]

Post-war policy in Cyprus, as elsewhere, saw the far right rehabilitated, even Nazi collaborators, as part of an anti-communist coalition.

Despite Woolley also receiving support from the advisory council, which by joining Triantafyllides had triggered the extremists against him, Stanley rejected his proposal on 25 June 1945. It was too risky to return the fanatical Makarios.[34] Yet, Makarios told Loizides in Athens that the British would soon permit his return as part of a Anglo-Hellenic anti-communist struggle.[35] Indeed Atlee's Labour government removed the restrictions on the deportees in October 1946, coinciding with Lord Winster, a Labour peer, being made governor.[36] Makarios returned on 22 December 1946 and within two weeks the British authorities reported that he was 'quite senile' and would need a deputy, which he got when he was archbishop.[37] In February 1947 the British government announced that it had no plans to cede Cyprus to Greece. Leontios and Clerides were part of a delegation to London at the time, and Makarios and

---

[32] FCO141/2617, minutes, executive council, 27 February 1945. Katsiaounis, 'Cyprus 1931–1959: The Politics of the Anti-Colonial Movement'.
[33] FCO141/2677, secret, Woolley to Stanley, 31 March 1945.
[34] FCO141/2677, secret, Stanley to Woolley, 25 June 1945; Ibid., minutes of advisory council, May 1945.
[35] FCO141/2617, Loizides to Ioannides, 14 May 1946.
[36] FCO141/2677, Extraordinary Gazette, 29 October 1946; Ibid., CSC to CCCP, 29 October 1946.
[37] FCO141/2617, telegram, GoC to CO, 23 December 1946; Ibid., DCNic to CSC, 3 January 1947; FCO141/4281, top secret, KEK Dossier, 1949.

his supporters organised a 'protest rally', for which permission was given, but the District Commissioner of Nicosia had prophetic reservations over giving future permission:

> I should like to take this opportunity of recording in writing my view that if we continue to issue permits for seditious meetings there can be only one ultimate end – bloodshed. It may not come tomorrow, indeed I do not think it will. It may not come this year, but sooner or later some unforeseen provocation will come about, there will be disorders and it will be necessary to fire shots.[38]

Makarios was transmitted through loud speakers to a small crowd of less than 10,000. After a prayer, he launched into a historical diatribe on the myth that the British were welcomed by Archbishop Sophronios with the desire of *enosis* but they had been repeatedly disappointed. He bemoaned his exile and the occupation, and that the Cypriot people had supported the allies, not disclosing, of course, his own collaborationist history. He asked the people to keep faith, to remain devoted Christians, a clear attack on communism, and to support the King of Greece, and together, through Anglo-Greek friendship, they would achieve *enosis*.[39] The decision to allow Makarios and his devotees to return opened a Pandora's box, bringing the militant politics of the Greek Civil War to Cyprus and making the formation of EOKA possible.

Makarios's return coincided with the formation of 'Organisation X' in Cyprus by Euripides Zemenides, a dentist and brother of Angelos, in 1946. This followed its collapse in Greece: in early 1945 the British estimated that 'X' had 200,000 men, but at the 1946 elections it won less than 0.2 per cent. In Cyprus they were active in 1947, especially after Leontios died, in supporting Bishop Makarios for archbishop by threatening AKEL leaders and members. He funded their newspapers: Polycarpos Ioannides published *Εφημερίς* (Newspaper) in Kyrenia from July 1946 and Evagoras Papa Nicolaou *Εσπερινή-Πρωτεύουσα* (Evening-Capital) in Nicosia. Former EREK members were its nucleus and it formed the nucleus of EOKA.[40]

---

[38] FCO141/2978, Arthur, District Commissioner of Nicosia and Kyrenia, to CSC, 15 February 1947.

[39] FCO141/2978, secret, Ashmore, Commissioner of Police, to CSC, 17 February 1947.

[40] FCO141/4281, top secret, KEK Dossier, 1949; Katsiaounis, *Η Διασκεπτική*, 287; Kousouris, *Δίκες τών Δοσίλογων*, 194–95; Alecou, *Communism and Nationalism in Postwar Cyprus*, 84–89. Euripides's son Angelos was a candidate for Takis Evdokas's far-right

In June 1947, Leontios was 'elected' Archbishop with the support of AKEL, but he died of typhus and complications with diabetes, so the British claimed, within 5 weeks.[41] There is a widespread rumour that he was poisoned, perhaps emanating from the fact that his body did not lie in state as was custom, recently the subject of a fictional account by Sophronis Sophroniou, *Οι Πρωτόπλαστοι* (The Protagonists).[42] The case is as mysterious as that of Triantafyllides's assassination 13 years earlier. Typhus was the official cause of death, yet nobody else connected to Leontios contracted typhus, which is highly contagious. Katsiaounis revealed that Leontios died after several days of illness, that the doctors were unsure of a diagnosis or treatment (typhus has common symptoms, i.e., fever, headache and rash), and that Ploutis Servas, a former General Secretary of the CPC (1936–41) and AKEL (1941–45) and Mayor of Limassol (1943–49), told him that he believed that his death was not from natural causes.[43] Clearly it was suspicious, but who and why? Three groups had opportunity and motive. Ezekias Papaioannou, a Cypriot communist in London from the early 1930s, back in Cyprus from January 1946 and elected General Secretary of AKEL in August 1949, believed that the British poisoned or infected Leontios with typhus.[44] This is possible, though unlikely. The British disliked Leontios, especially his efforts to unite the Left and Right behind *enosis* because it meant cooperating with AKEL. But Winster had only arrived in October 1946 with instructions to pursue constitutional reform and assassinating Leontios meant that the British were willing to accept his likely successor, Makarios. Moreover, one could also accuse the Americans, who were negotiating to move their Foreign Broadcast Information Service (branch of CIA) from Cairo to Cyprus when Leontios died.[45] But the most suspicious actions surround doctors from Greece attending Leontios, who Cypriot doctors accused of failing to administer the necessary drugs, which were available at the Government Hospital,[46] and the actions of 'X' and KEK, with Dervis

---

party in the 1970 elections. See http://www.papademetris.net/index.php?option=com_content&view=article&id=2414:s-1852&catid=219:1967-1972-10&Itemid=124

[41] *The Times*, 28 July 1947, 3.
[42] Stamelos, 'A Case Study of State and Law', 77.
[43] Katsiaounis, *Η Διασκεπτική*, 276–77. In his memoirs, Servas said nothing. Ploutis Servas, *Κυπριακό: Ευθύνες* [Cyprus Problem: Responsibilities] (Athens: Grammi, 1980), 145.
[44] Ezekias Papaioannou, *Ενθυμήσεις από την Ζωή Μου* [Memories from My Life] (Nicosia: Pirsos, 1988), 79–81.
[45] CIA-RDP80, A. A. Dudley to McIntyre, American Embassy, 8 July 1947; CIA-RDP80, Chief FBIS to Frost, 8 August 1947.
[46] *West Australian*, 7 August 1947, 10; *Daily Mercury*, 7 August 1947, 1.

being one of Leontios's doctors, along with two other right-wing figures, Nicholas Iakovides and Ioannis Spyridakis.[47]

One author described what followed Leontios's death as 'a coup'.[48] By December 1947, Makarios was archbishop. Dervis was triumphant, telling the media: 'This victory is a slap in Britain's face. Makarios was among the leaders of the 1931 rising. He made himself conspicuous by tearing the Union Jack from Government buildings and spitting on it. He will lead us again now towards *enosis*'.[49] Also triumphant were Makarios's coterie of Savvas Loizides, who returned to Cyprus until September 1948, Ioannides, and Papa Nicolaou.[50] As soon as Leontios died, Makarios, now the *locum tenens*, and his coterie, moved into the Archbishopric and took measures to ensure that Makarios was the next archbishop.[51] These included the excommunication and removal of left-wingers from ecclesiastical electoral roles, rejection of the Consultative Assembly, bombardment of the island from Radio Athens with programmes supporting Makarios in the upcoming elections, to stinging attacks on the British authorities, and finally the open use of 'Organisation X' in Cyprus.[52] As these measures were taken within 10 days of Leontios's death, they were planned in advance. While four months earlier AKEL support had easily led Leontios to victory, now the far right easily had Makarios elected, winning 47 of the 66 general representatives, with the three lay representatives in Nicosia being none other than Dervis, Zemenides and Dr Miltiades Coureas.[53]

Was it possible that those who seemingly had Triantafyllides assassinated in 1934 also had Leontios assassinated in 1947? Was it coincidental that Loizides, Ioannides, Papa Nicolaou, and Makarios were in Cyprus in 1947, and Dervis and Coureas were now staunch Makarios supporters? The evidence is less conclusive, yet opportunity and motives existed, with the motives being as

---

[47] See http://www.papademetris.net/index.php?option=com_content&view =article&id=1340:s-783&catid=126:1945-1949-6&Itemid=116

[48] Andreas Panayiotou, "Πως Εξαφανίζεται η Ιστορία: Το Πραξικόπημα του Κατεστημένου τον Ιούλιο του 1947 και οι Ρίζες του Ελληνοκυπριακού Βαθέως Κράτους της Δεξιάς" [How History Disappears: The Coup d'état of July 1947 and the Roots of the Deep Right-Wing Greek Cypriot State], forthcoming.

[49] *Mercury*, 1 November 1947, 1.

[50] Coudounaris, *Βιογραφικόν Λεξικόν Κυπρίων*, 285.

[51] See FCO141/2976; Fifis Ioannou, *Ετσι Ξεκίνησε το Κυπριακό: Στα Χνάρια μιας Δεκαετίας, 1940–1950* [Thus Began the Cyprus Conflict: In the Footsteps of a Decade, 1940–1950] (Athens: Filistor, 2005), 249; Katsiaounis, *Η Διασκεπτική*, 211–26, 276–87.

[52] FCO141/4281, top secret, KEK Dossier, 1949; Papaioannou, *Ενθυμήσεις από την Ζωή Μου*, 86, 91–93; Katsiaounis, *Η Διασκεπτική*, 212, 249–55, 276–86, 403, 414–24, 486–95; Alecou, *Communism and Nationalism in Postwar Cyprus*, 78–89.

[53] See http://www.papademetris.net/index.php?option=com_content&view =article&id=1342:s-785&catid=127:1945-1949-7&Itemid=116

strong and quite similar to the assassination of Triantafyllides: at stake was the archiepiscopal throne and control of the national liberation struggle. As with Triantafyllides, Makarios supporters, specifically Ioannides and Papa Nicolaou, had attacked Leontios. The attacks were periodic in the 1930s,[54] but grew intense as Leontios wanted a united pro-*enosis* front from across the ideological spectrum. But working with the communists and the step-by-step approach to *enosis* of AKEL, the centre-left and centre-right, angered the far right. Thus, by wanting unity on *enosis*, Leontios became the enemy of the far right. His switch to a far right position while on his deathbed, possibly under pressure and even threat from the extremist Makarios supporters, did not save him.[55] But the fanaticism of the far right found fertile ground within KEK, which, as British intelligence argued in 1949, was the only strong right-wing bulwark against communism.[56]

Nevertheless, as the epigraph shows, numerous Cypriots involved in public life had centrist views, but were muscled aside by the far right and far left. After the assassination of Triantafyllides, Clerides, Cacoyannis and Vassiliades, referring to the smooth running of the advisory council, called for a new constitution, but were thwarted by Palmer and the Colonial Office.[57] Clerides and Vassiliades were centre-left. Vassiliades was a founding member of AKEL in 1941, which Servas looked to model on the British Labour Party until the Stalinists removed him as leader in 1945. Other centre-left figures included Fifis Ioannou, AKEL General-Secretary, 1945–49, Lysos Santamas, a lawyer and Mayor of Larnaca, 1946–53, Adam Adamantos, a teacher and Mayor of Famagusta, 1943–53, and Polycarpos Nikopoulos, Mayor of Morphou, 1943–69. Clerides defeated Dervis for Mayor of Nicosia in 1946 with AKEL support and headed AKEL's National Liberation Coalition (NLC) from September 1947 to promote self-government.[58] There were also many centre-right Cypriots, who, although anti-communist, did not share the inflexibility of KEK on self-government and its flirtation with the far right. As one stated to Parkinson (epigraph), they feared being branded as 'traitors'.[59] They remembered the assassination of Triantafyllides, because, like him, they were willing to work with the government to develop Cyprus.[60] Despite

---

[54] CO67/254/3, secret, Palmer to Cunliffe-Lister, 22 June 1934.
[55] Alecou, *Communism and Nationalism in Postwar Cyprus*, 62–63.
[56] FCO141/4281, top secret, KEK Dossier, 1949.
[57] Rappas, *Cyprus in the 1930s*, 88–122.
[58] Leventis, *Cyprus*, 196–210; Alecou, *Communism and Nationalism in Postwar Cyprus*, 26–29.
[59] FCO141/2874, Thomas, CO, to Reddaway, 31 October 1944, with anonymous to Parkinson, 1 September 1944.
[60] FCO141/4281, top secret, KEK Dossier, 1949.

the death of Paschalis and Cacoyannis's retirement in 1946 (aged only 53), others promoted right-wing centrist views. One group worked *in* the government, such as Stelios Pavlides, the Attorney General (1944–52), member of the executive and advisory councils, and Criton Tornaritis, Solicitor General (1944–52) and later Attorney General (1952–56). Others worked *with* the government, including Paul G. Pavlides, member of the executive council, George Aradippiotis, Mayor of Larnaca, 1932–43, George Chrysafinis, member of the executive council, 1946–52 and lawyer (son of Nicholas Chrysafinis and his daughter married Antis Triantafyllides), Socrates E. Evangelides, lawyer and member of the advisory council (1942–45), and Constantine Fieros, lawyer and Mayor of Kyrenia, 1935–43. There were others such as Loizos Philippou, editor of *Πάφος*, and businessmen Demosthenis Severis, his sons Costas and Zenon, Panayiotis Tseriotis and Nicholas C. Lanitis. The Consultative Assembly did not unite enough of these centrists and failed for two additional reasons. First, as George Chrysafinis revealed in August 1947 to Winster, the far right and the Greek government spread the rumour that Athens and Whitehall had almost agreed on *enosis* and that the Consultative Assembly would jeopardise these talks: 'If I did not already possess confidential information as a member of the executive council, I would have succumbed to this expectation myself'. Leontios had succumbed to this propaganda three days before his death under pressure from Makarios. The Consultative Assembly then collapsed because the centre-left delegates (Clerides, Servas, Santamas, Adamantos and Nikopoulos) failed to convince the British to grant responsible self-government and rejected the proposed constitution, which resembled that offered to Triantafyllides in 1921. AKEL consolidated communist control and destroyed the NLC, with numerous centre-left figures expelled or resigning, including Servas, Adamantos, Ioannou, Santamas and Nikopoulos from 1948 to 1952, dropping support for Clerides for the Mayorship of Nicosia in 1949, and, after consulting the Greek communist leadership, adopted *enosis* and only *enosis* in 1949.[61] Nevertheless, Chrysafinis, Ioannou and Clerides (then in the executive council) united as late as 1953 to call for a constitution that would lead to self-government.[62]

The centre-right watched KEK and 'X' refuse to consider constitutional reforms, believing that the British would deliver *enosis* to secure an anti-communist coalition with Greece. The leaders of KEK were 'bigoted, unconstructive and uncooperative' and 'parrot-like' in repeating their 'totally

---

[61] T. W. Adams, *AKEL the Communist Party of Cyprus* (Stanford: Hoover Institute, 1971), 142, 157; Katsiaounis, *Η Διασκεπτική*, 270–71; Leventis, *Cyprus*, 196–210; Alecou, *Communism and Nationalism in Postwar Cyprus*, 62–64, 89–93, 119–30, 132–34.

[62] Stefanides, *Isle of Discord*, 242.

unpractical slogan of *enosis* and only *enosis*'.⁶³ In January 1947, Kolokasides and Tsangarides returned to Athens via Cairo where they met the Cypriot diaspora who told the British High Commissioner that they were fanatics opposed to self-government and feared a communist uprising in Cyprus which could only be stopped by *enosis*.⁶⁴ As Ioannides stated in *Εφιμερίς* in April 1948: '*Enosis* and only *enosis*: Until it is achieved we prefer to be ruled by England, but we do not accept power in the hands of the people'. Predictably, right-wing bishops, supported by KEK and 'X', were elected to the three vacant bishoprics in 1948, after the purge of the electoral lists of left-wingers. Next 'X' ordered employers to dismiss left-wingers or face a boycott of their businesses, and Ioannides ramped up his attacks on moderates; he was imprisoned for three months in February 1949 for libelling Clerides in *Εφιμερίς*. In September 1948 the ethnarchy council, which Leontios had established in July 1945 as an all-party body but by 1948 was only representative of the far right, created an Athens office, which consisted of none other than Loizides (director), Tsangarides and Kolokasides.⁶⁵ Unsurprisingly, Dervis won the Mayorship of Nicosia, with Zemenides on his ticket becoming a councillor.⁶⁶

Then Archbishop Makarios II, through the newly elected Bishop of Kitium, also Makarios, organised a 'plebiscite'. The idea originated in 1935 with the deportees in Athens lobbying the League of Nations.⁶⁷ After the Second World War, AKEL proposed it, and it was acted upon by the right wing. Unsurprisingly, the far right had a warped sense of what a plebiscite and democracy were. The vote was an open ballot of signatures and was conducted in churches, with the two choices being: (1) 'We demand union with Greece' and (2) 'We are against the union of Cyprus with Greece'. Incredibly 4.3 per cent voted against. But the open ballot was not the only irregularity. Meant to be over one day, 15 January, but when too few voted, the registers remained open for a week, allowing for manipulation, while there were widespread reports of intimidation and force on those signing 'against' to re-sign in favour.⁶⁸

Makarios II died in June 1950, but his anti-communism, *enosis* and only *enosis* policy and confrontational style was adopted by his successor, the Bishop

---

[63] FCO141/4281, top secret, KEK Dossier, 1949.
[64] FCO141/2874, confidential, British Consulate Alexandria to British Embassy, Cairo, 17 January 1947.
[65] Loizides, *Άτυχη Κύπρος*, 54; Leventis, *Cyprus*, 171–72; Katsourides, *Greek Cypriot Nationalist Right*, 196–97.
[66] http://www.papademetris.net/index.php?option=com_content&view=article&id=1342:s-785&catid=127:1945-1949-7&Itemid=116
[67] *The Straits Times*, 26 January 1935, 6.
[68] George Horton Kelling, *Countdown to Rebellion: British Policy in Cyprus, 1939–1955* (New York: Greenwood, 1990), 103–4.

of Kitium, who became Makarios III in October 1950.⁶⁹ Within months he agreed to the proposal, made by none other than Loizides and his brother Socrates (whom Makarios had been to school with), at a meeting in Athens in March 1951, that a secret group in Athens and consisting of the brothers and former Greek military figures would coordinate an armed struggle against the British to achieve *enosis* and recruit Grivas to lead it. In his memoirs, Loizides admitted:

> For me, obviously, the idea was an old one. Because it was this idea that was at the core of the secret Organisation of the National Radical Union in 1930, which was tied to the spontaneous national revolt of 1931 [...]⁷⁰

Where EREK had failed to use political violence in 1931, EOKA would succeed, with a clear line of dissent between them.

Having convinced Makarios to support an armed struggle, the Loizides brothers recruited Grivas in May 1951 to lead it. Grivas, as stated earlier, a collaborator with the Nazi occupiers and collaborationist regime, was tossed aside after the war by the Greek right wing that no longer needed his militancy. He visited Cyprus in summer 1951 for a reconnaissance mission and to consult with Makarios. Finally, in July 1952, Savvas Loizides, having formed a 'secret committee' in Athens, organised a meeting with Makarios and Grivas, when it was agreed that Makarios would lead the political struggle and Grivas the military one.⁷¹ Then on 7 March 1953, Loizides organised another meeting in Athens, where the 12 members (including Makarios and Grivas) of the secret committee signed an oath, reminiscent of EREK's oath of 1931.

> I swear in the name of the Holy Trinity to dedicate and sacrifice even my own life, suffering the harshest of tortures, to keep secret that I know and desire the Union of Cyprus, and will blindly obey all orders in connection therein.⁷²

Thus, Loizides, one of the leaders of EREK and probably one of the planners of the assassination of Triantafyllides, was also instrumental in

---

⁶⁹ Ibid., 119–38; Stefanides, *Isle of Discord*, 17.
⁷⁰ Loizides, *Άτυχη Κύπρος*, 96–97. Grivas, *Memoirs of General Grivas*, 13.
⁷¹ Loizides, *Άτυχη Κύπρος*, 96–100. Grivas, *Memoirs of General Grivas*, 13–32. Grivas claimed that the idea of an 'armed struggle' originated with him back in May 1948, but there is no evidence.
⁷² Loizides, *Άτυχη Κύπρος*, 96–100.

forming EOKA. From 1951 to 1955, Loizides, then a municipal councillor in Athens, was the middleman between Makarios, Grivas and the Greek authorities sponsoring EOKA and published several pro-*enosis* propaganda pieces. Then, as an MP in Athens for ERE from 1956 to 1958, he represented Greece at the UN during debates on Cyprus, and embarrassed the Greek government, perhaps explaining why he did not run in the 1958 elections, by being the only member of the Greek delegation to reject independence, angrily declaring in the chamber that his patience for *enosis* had run out in 1931 and that he would not return to Cyprus to live there, preferring to 'live in exile' (although he was free to live in Cyprus) in Greece.[73]

But he was not the only former EREK member and likely mastermind of Triantafyllides's assassination to have played a role in EOKA. Polycarpos Ioannides was exiled to the Seychelles with Makarios III in 1956.[74] Ioannides and the Kyrenia Diocese under Bishop Kyprianos remained stubborn fanatics opposed to the Zurich–London Accords that were the basis of the Republic of Cyprus. So much so that Ioannides supported the anti-Makarios coalition consisting of Dervis, as the leader of the Democratic Union, and AKEL, in supporting Ioannis Clerides for President in the December 1959 presidential elections.[75] During the campaign, Ioannides called Makarios 'the undertaker of the Cypriot people' for accepting independence.[76] There was some irony in this, since Clerides, who had spoken so beautifully at the funeral of Triantafyllides, had consistently supported self-government, and had been the last Greek Cypriot to resign from the executive council in 1956 in protest at the deportation of Makarios, Ioannides and Kyprianos, was now being supported in the first Cypriot presidential elections by those who seemingly orchestrated Triantafyllides's assassination 25 years earlier.

---

[73] See Savvas Loizides, *The Cyprus Question: Its Evolution – Present Aspects after the Plebiscite of January 1950* (Nicosia, 1950); Savvas Loizides, 'The Cyprus Question in the United Nations', *Revue Hellenique de Droit International* 7 (1954): 214–19; Savvas Loizides, *Cyprus demands Self-Determination* (Athens: National Committee for Self-Determination of Cyprus, 1956). Xydis, Stephen, *Cyprus: Conflict and Conciliation, 1954–1958* (Columbus: Ohio State University, 1967), 58–60, 380–81, 391–99. In 1956, the name National Radical Union replaced Greek Rally as the name of the ruling right-wing party in Greece, led then by the new prime minister, Constantine Karamanlis, which was essentially the same name as Loizides's National Radical Union of Cyprus (EREK).

[74] For Ioannides see French, *Fighting EOKA*, 104.

[75] Clerides (who polled a strong 33.3%) formed the Democratic Union with his archenemy Dervis because he believed that the Zurich–London Accords would militarise Cyprus, further divide Greek and Turkish Cypriots, and lead to a Makarios dictatorship. Crawshaw, *The Cyprus Revolt*, 354–55.

[76] *Daily Express*, 7 December 1959, 2.

The failure to punish those seemingly responsible for the assassination of Triantafyllides meant that they simply bided their time until they were rehabilitated, which they were after the Second World War because of their anti-communism. For them violence was the only way, hence the formation of EOKA. In the process, they swept aside other methods by which *enosis* could be obtained, bringing to the archiepiscopal throne Bishop Makarios, possibly after murdering his predecessor, and instituting their *enosis* and *enosis* policy, which had been repeatedly viewed by many educated Cypriots with scepticism and concern.

As for *enosis*, these fanatics claimed to represent the pro-*enosis* demands of the population, especially the peasants, yet two reports from Greek Cypriots bring this into question. In September 1953 a newly appointed Greek Cypriot District Inspector in Famagusta revealed that *enosis* lacked peasant support.

> The overwhelming majority of the peasants do not have the intelligentsia's sentimental attachment to *Enosis*. What they chiefly care about is peace, order, good administration and a satisfactory standard of living as they have known it in the last 10 or 15 years.[77]

Meanwhile, in London, the Cypriot Commissioner of the Cyprus Government London Office, Phaedon Constantinides, stated in February 1958 that 90 per cent or more of the Cypriots in the Greater London area were of peasant and labouring stock 'of a very low intellectual level and semi-literate' and so were 'influenced by clever political vagabonds'. Importantly, most of the Cypriots in the UK were law-abiding and simply trying to get on with their lives and 'fail to understand why in the heart of London there is an open and systematic anti-British propaganda being carried on' by a small minority of far right and left-wing pro-*enosis* supporters.[78]

With the adoption of violence by EOKA and the failure to achieve *enosis*, one must seriously question the path taken by the extremists from 1934 and the control they exerted over the national liberation struggle from 1947, since they seemingly assassinated Triantafyllides when he and others offered an alternative route to *enosis* or liberation, which could have also achieved independence, but without the violence and its divisive ramifications.

---

[77] FCO141/2874, secret, DCFam to CSC, 8 September 1953, enclosing report by D. Paralikis, District Inspector Famagusta, 5 September 1953.

[78] FCO141/4198, top secret, Constantinides to Sheridan, Administrative Secretary's Office, Cyprus, 12 February 1958.

CONCLUSION

Oh very young, what will you leave us this time.
'Oh Very Young', music and lyrics by Cat Stevens, from *Buddha and the Chocolate Box*, 1974.

My father died in 2019 when I was 39. I cannot imagine what my life would have been like had I lost him aged 7, when Michalakis Triantafyllides lost his father Antonios and his brothers were even younger. While being interviewed at 75, he cried uncontrollably as he recollected how his idyllic childhood was destroyed that fateful evening when his father was shot. He was in the house with his mother and brothers, when they heard the shots and a maid rushed in with the tragic news.[1] The family were fortunately taken in by their aunt and uncle (Maria and Stelios Pavlides), yet they had lost a husband and father, an irreplaceable part of their lives, and he missed seeing them grow into upstanding members of society. And the nation lost a son. A man of intelligence, integrity and political acumen beyond most Cypriots then and since, and as Blackall stated: 'he was the most statesmanlike figure among the Greek Cypriots'.[2] Antonios Triantafyllides was not merely a once in a generation politician for Cyprus, but a once in a lifetime one.

The analysis of the evidence has shown that there existed a far right, specifically fascist, pro-*enosis* faction anxious to address the dilution of the nationalist pro-*enosis* ranks and *enosis* and only *enosis* stance with violence, thus highlighting the ambiguities in the prosecution of Cypriot nationalist and pro-*enosis* politics during the interwar years. Evidence pointed to a group of extremist nationalists, with fascist tendencies, some deported after the October 1931 disturbances and living in Athens and others still in Cyprus, as masterminding the assassination. This was the original view of Palmer, Blackall and Paschalis, and five of them were interned, including Dr Pigasiou, named as the mastermind by crown witnesses, contrary to the crown's communist conspiracy. This

---

[1] Michalakis Triantafyllides interview, 1 February 2002, in Solomonidou-Drousiotou, *Η Ζωή μου σε Πρώτο Πρόσωπο*, 33–41.
[2] MSS Brit Emp s447, Blackall papers, notes beneath translated article from *Πατρίς*.

was reinforced by the evidence from Theodotou and Surridge; by the writings in the Athenian newspapers from the deportees to establish the 'personal motive' theory to deny the assassination; and by the threatening letters received by other Greek Cypriots either nominated or elected to represent the people.

Therefore, the most likely scenario for who masterminded and executed the assassination of Triantafyllides is as follows:

- The decision was taken by the deported EREK figures in Athens, namely Savvas Loizides, Theophanis Tsangarides, Theodoros Kolokasides and Makarios, Bishop of Kyrenia.
- They ordered their associates in Cyprus, Dr Ioannis Pigasiou, Evagoras Papa Nicolaou, and Polycarpos Ioannides, to pay someone to shoot Triantafyllides. Ioannides, the secretary of the Kyrenia Diocese organised the payment. Pigasiou knew Stavros Christodoulou as he had worked for him. Loizides was from the same village as Christodoulou. Three prosecution witnesses testified in court, contrary to the case of the prosecution, that Pigasiou had paid Christodoulou to shoot Triantafyllides.
- Triantafyllides may have been selected randomly, as suggested by Michalakis Triantafyllides, but there is no evidence to support this and it would seem more likely that Antonios was selected because he was the most despised and for maximum impact against cooperation with the British.
- Using reverse psychology, the men seemingly responsible, unlike the rest of Cyprus, which was shocked, saddened and disgusted, celebrated the assassination. They publicly stated that Triantafyllides deserved to die, thus revealing their motives to have organised it. Meanwhile, they tried to confuse the investigation and public by inventing the personal motive theory, which also aimed at destroying Triantafyllides's reputation.
- Those behind the assassination had a predisposition to violence. They had wanted to use violence in 1931, they were possibly behind two other assassinations and, those still alive, were instrumental in forming EOKA in the 1950s.

Their motives were clear: they considered Triantafyllides a traitor for cooperating with the British and for opposing their fanatical views. Specifically, they were angered by and hated him because:

- They had supported his election to the legislative council in 1930, but, in their eyes, he betrayed their support by accepting the British invitation to join the executive council.

- During the 1931 crisis he had argued for restraint to prevent conflict with the British, angering those who seemingly planned his assassination, who were pushing for a violent clash.
- He supported the view of Greek Prime Minister Eleftherios Venizelos, whom they also despised, that the best path towards achieving *enosis* or liberation was to work with the British to develop the economy, society and politics of the island, so that the Cypriot people were ready to support a movement for *enosis* or liberation and convince the British and the Turkish Cypriots that *enosis* or liberation was feasible and desirable.
- He joined the advisory council announced in October 1933, for which they attacked him viciously, by reasoning that it was a necessary step to re-establish better relations with the British before a constitution could be reintroduced, and before any thought of prosecuting a movement for *enosis* or liberation.
- He advised after the death of Archbishop Kyrillos III in November 1933 that, according to the statutes of the Cypriot Orthodox Church, the election of a new archbishop could take place without the physical presence of the two deported bishops (Makarios and Nicodemos) and, after they disagreed with this legal assessment, he advised that they should resign to facilitate the election.
- He was intelligent, logical and popular with the general population and other educated elites, and if he succeeded in overseeing the development of the economy, society and politics of the island, the people might not want *enosis* with a weak and poor Greece and instead prefer an alternative, such as self-government and independence.

The scholarly significance of this study to British imperial and colonial history is immense because:

- It serves as a model for exploring other assassinations/attempted assassinations in and beyond the British Empire, for it is a model of forensic analysis of cold cases.
- It complicates the widely held view that resistance to the British Empire means resistance at all times, when there are different forms of challenge, opposition and resistance, including cooperation to strengthen a community to call for more rights and liberty.
- The assassination shows that the British were too weak to protect those willing to work with them to develop the country and lead it towards self-government and liberation. This weakness was not a security failure, but a failure of political strategy, which should have aimed at developing a

broader collective cooperation, rather than the selective one adopted (four-member advisory council), which exposed Triantafyllides and others.
- The British believed that communist-led anti-colonialism was a greater threat than far right anti-colonialism to the degree that they switched from a far right conspiracy to assassinate Triantafyllides to a communist-led one. There is even a possibility of a British cover-up and collusion to protect the likely far right perpetrators. Then the likely perpetrators of the assassination of Triantafyllides were rehabilitated after the Second World War to join an 'anti-communist coalition', and were therefore free to adopt political violence, helping to form EOKA. As a consequence, the British seemingly played a significant part in paving the way for the formation of EOKA and its use of political violence, by not punishing the likely perpetrators of the assassination of Triantafyllides and then allowing them to play a prominent role in the politics of Cyprus after the Second World War.
- As unlikely as it seems that the British would have been involved in a conspiracy to cover up an assassination, particularly of an ally (of sorts), it seems just as unlikely that they would not have known who was behind an assassination that occurred anywhere in their empire. As this case shows, it seems likely that they knew who masterminded the assassination of Triantafyllides. They prosecuted the right person, but got the conspiracy behind it wrong.
- Despite efforts to demolish the colonial archive, it remains the most significant depository for reconstructing the colonial past, yet its significance and value depend on reading it both with and particularly against the grain.

The implications for Cypriot historical consciousness and historiography are unnerving for reasons that have contemporary resonance because the assassination:

- Could be the first in the name of *enosis*, 20 years before EOKA started its armed struggle (or the second, if Zemenides was assassinated for his anti-*enosis* activities in London). Thus, political violence originated before EOKA and was left to fester and return after the Second World War (possibly assassinating Archbishop Leontios), resulting in the formation of EOKA, including by the same men seemingly behind the assassination of Triantafyllides.
- Marks a key moment in modern Cypriot history, when cooperation with the colonial power may have avoided the bloody violence that characterised the later colonial period, by instituting a new constitutional process. This is not a far-fetched scenario given that many educated elites supported and continued to support the views of Triantafyllides in judging that the best

way forward for *enosis* or liberation was a step-by-step one to transition the island from British rule.³ This was the successful strategy followed in Malta, despite multiple constitutional crises during the interwar years.
- Irrevocably impacted upon relations between moderate Greek Cypriot elites and the government. It became difficult for moderate Greek Cypriots, whether centre-left or centre-right, to organise politically for fear of being struck down by far right extremists. It also became difficult for the British government to promote a constitutional path (at least not until after the war) or moderate political parties, for fear that Greek Cypriot supporters would be ostracised, threatened or even assassinated.
- Created fear among politicians and elites that supported the approach of Triantafyllides, preventing the development of an organised political alternative to the far right and far left anti-imperial/colonial projects. The fear was ever-present because of the failure to punish those seemingly behind the assassination of Triantafyllides and their rehabilitation after the Second World War to join the 'coalition' against communism.
- Resulted in Cypriot politics being increasingly influenced and controlled by militant far right forces.⁴ True centre-right and centre-left parties never developed, partly because of the control of the far right and far left, and, sometimes, the populist 'nationalist' so-called 'centre'. The right wing joined the far right, giving it legitimacy with the faces first of Dervis, Makarios II, and later Makarios III, while adopting far right intransigence over *enosis* and later Turkish Cypriot rights. They eventually took the centre-right with them, simply because the only other alternative, AKEL, was too radically left wing. EOKA's violence was followed by postcolonial state and parastate violence, aimed mainly at the Turkish Cypriots, until the Greek Cypriots turned on each other after Makarios III announced in 1967 that independence was the feasible policy as opposed to the desirable policy of *enosis*, and was attacked (including multiple assassination attempts) by the far right, leading to EOKA B and the coup that toppled him in 1974. After the 1974 war, Glafkos Clerides, the son of Ioannis Clerides, founded Democratic Rally, with broad-minded and Western-orientated intellectuals and a pragmatic view on reunifying the island, but it incorporated most of the far right, which it mostly still relies upon to win power. Consequently, the far right and far right maximalist positions, first on *enosis* and now reunification, have played and continue to play an important role in government and politics.

---

³ Rappas, *Cyprus in the 1930s*, 88–122.
⁴ Alecou, *Communism and Nationalism in Postwar Cyprus*, 75.

Many historians cringe at hypotheticals, yet we should use our expertise to imagine how events may have unfolded differently after a turning point such as the assassination of Triantafyllides. So, what *could* the history of Cyprus have been had he not been assassinated?

- While Stefanides claimed that Cyprus could never have taken a constitutional path,[5] the support for such a path was widespread amongst Cypriot intellectuals (both inside and outside the colonial bureaucracy), and therefore a real possibility had Triantafyllides lived. So, after two years of successful functioning and cooperation, Triantafyllides convinces the Colonial Office to dissolve the advisory council and announce a new constitution with a legislative assembly, similar to the Maltese one (introduced in 1936 after the three-year suspension of the previous one) and previous Cypriot one (15 elected members – 12 Christians and 3 Muslims). Elections are held in 1936, which barred clerics and foreign nationals from running.
- To fight the election, Triantafyllides forms a centre-right-wing party, perhaps called 'Liberal National Party of Cyprus', based on liberalism, pragmatism, and liberal-conservatism, attracting liberals, conservatives, moderate nationalists and peasants/farmers.
- In response, Ioannis Clerides forms a centre-left-wing party, perhaps called 'Cypriot Labour Party', based on the British Labour Party, to contest the elections, attracting left-wing intellectuals, and middle- and working-class people. It also forms trade unions.
- These two parties attract the best and brightest minds, including Panayiotis Cacoyiannis, Nicholas Chrysafinis, George Chrysafinis, Demosthenis Severis, Zenon Severis, Costas Severis, Neoptolemos Paschalis, Stavros Stavrinakis, Adam Adamantos, Stelios Pavlides, Stavros Stavrinides, Ploutis Servas, Paul Pavlides, Demetris N. Demetriou, George Aradippiotis, George Vassiliades, Lysos Santamas, Polycarpos Nikolopoulos, Fifis Ioannou, Costas Ashiotis, Panayiotis Tseriotis, Criton Tornaritis, Constantine Fieros and even Themistocles Dervis and many others, and eventually the sons of Triantafyllides and Clerides, Michalakis and Glafkos respectively. Hereafter these two personalities and parties dominate Cypriot politics (like George Borg Olivier and his Nationalist Party and Dom Mintoff's Labour Party in Malta).
- The far right and communists are marginalised into small groups of diehards. Meanwhile, the Cypriot Orthodox Church, like the Maltese Catholic Church, which had played a similar role in politics during the

---

[5] Stefanides, *Isle of Discord*, 242.

interwar years, was no longer seriously involved in politics, with supporters splitting between both major parties.
- In 1945 Triantafyllides and Clerides realise that with the progress made under constitutional government and the Greek Civil War raging, independence is the best future for Cyprus. They argue that this decision does not change the identity of Greek Cypriots as Greeks. They convince Turkish Cypriots to join them in their parties, with one elected as a vice president in each, and to trust in a future independent Cyprus. *Enosis*, like Italian irredentism in Malta, was dead.
- In 1946, after 10 years of successful functioning and after the significant contribution of Cypriots in the Second World War, a new constitution gave Cyprus self-government, with an expanded legislature (30 members – 24 Christians and 6 Muslims) that legislated on all affairs except foreign and defence, with a prime minister.
- In the first elections, Clerides triumphed with 13 Christians and 3 Muslims (16), as opposed to 11 Christians and 3 Muslims (14), and became prime minister.
- In the 1950 elections, Triantafyllides won, reversing the results from 1946.
- After eight years of successful functioning, in 1954 Triantafyllides and Clerides again united, this time to demand Cypriot independence. The British agreed to grant independence in 1955, provided that they leased two bases for 50 years, which was accepted.
- A constitutional assembly, consisting of Greek and Turkish Cypriots, and British constitutional experts, devised a constitution, whereby Cyprus became a constitutional monarchy, modelled on the Westminster system, with an assembly of 50 members (15 in Nicosia, 9 in Famagusta, 8 in Limassol, 6 in Larnaca, 6 in Paphos and 3 in Kyrenia, and 3 from the smaller demographic minority groups from across all of Cyprus), elected by the STV system with separate lists electing 35 Greek Cypriots (10 in Nicosia, 7 in Famagusta, 7 in Limassol, 5 in Larnaca, 4 in Paphos and 2 in Kyrenia), 12 Turkish Cypriots (5 in Nicosia, 2 in Famagusta, 1 in Limassol, 1 in Larnaca, 2 in Paphos and 1 in Kyrenia), and one each for the Maronite, Armenian and Roman Catholic communities. Independents could run, but no parties could field candidates unless both Greek and Turkish Cypriots were listed (except on the Maronite, Armenian and Latin electoral roles) and a government could only form if it had a minimum of 5 Turkish Cypriots (elected with the ruling party or as part of a coalition).
- In the first elections in 1955, Triantafyllides, aged 65, was elected prime minister, as his Liberal-Nationals won 19 Greek Cypriot seats, 6 Turkish Cypriot seats and the Armenian and Roman Catholic seats, for a total of 27. Aged 68, Clerides and his Labour Party won 15 Greek Cypriot seats,

6 Turkish Cypriot seats and the Maronite seat, for a total of 22. The communist party won 1 Greek Cypriot seat.
- Upon independence, Cyprus remained within the Commonwealth, and therefore the Queen remained the head of state.

This is wishful, yet not far-fetched. If Triantafyllides in 1934 had predicted the partition of Cyprus in 1974, or even the outbreak of violence in 1955, he would have been accused of exaggeration. The hypothetical scenario illustrates how his assassination changed the course of Cypriot history: if not a 'turning point', certainly a 'moment' of major significance. While a constitutional path would probably have led to the death of *enosis*, as the far right feared, it also probably would have led to a peaceful decolonisation and postcolonial state, where minorities were protected and the majority was satisfied with the partnership state. Even if we look at what happened, in the post-1974 period several politicians emerged on both the Left (George Vassiliou, president, 1988–93) and Right (Alecos Markides, Attorney General, 1995–2003, and independent presidential candidate, 2003) who adopted the pragmatic politics of Triantafyllides.

In 1974 Cat Stevens/Yusuf Islam, the great English-Cypriot-Swedish singer-songwriter, sang his timeless words, 'Oh very young, what will you leave us this time?' Triantafyllides was assassinated too young, cut down in his prime, with much to offer his homeland, as many of his contemporaries commented on after his death. What he left 'us', not only Cypriots but anyone interested in politics, his legacy, as it were, has been hidden until now. Triantafyllides stood for the exact opposite of what those who seemingly organised his assassination and came to dominate the course of Cypriot politics did, pragmatism, negotiation, cooperation, adaptability, and above all, integrity. It might be too late for Cyprus to change its history, but it is never too late to change its current course, to bring about the reunification of this country. And it would certainly be a twist of fate if another Triantafyllides, and perhaps a woman, was to be that person.

SELECT BIBLIOGRAPHY

Primary Sources
Unpublished Documents
Central Intelligence Agency, USA

CIA-RDP

National Archives of the UK, Kew Gardens, London

Cabinet; Colonial Office; Foreign and Commonwealth Office ; Foreign Office.

Bodleian Library, Special Collections, University of Oxford

MSS Brit Emp s347, unpublished memoirs of Charles Frederic Belcher.
MSS Brit Emp s447, papers of Sir Henry William Blackall.
MSS Brit Emp s467, papers of Sir William Denis Battershill.

Cypriot State Archives, Nicosia

Secretariat Archive 1 (SA1).

Costas and Rita Severis Foundation: Centre of Visual Arts and Research (CVAR)

ARF 00284, Diary of Sir Henry Blackall.
ARF 01092, Diary of Rupert Gunnis.

University of Melbourne Microfilm Collection

Sir Ronald Storrs Papers, originals housed at Pembroke College, Cambridge.

Private Papers

Private Papers of Stelios A. Triantafyllides, Nicosia, Cyprus.

Official Published Documents

Cyprus Blue Book for 1935, Government Printing Office, Nicosia, 1936.
Cyprus Gazette 1934, British Colonial Government, Nicosia, 1934.
Cyprus Gazette 1935, British Colonial Government, Nicosia, 1935.
Cyprus: Report on the Cyprus Police Force for the Year 1934, by W. C. C. King, Government Printing Office, Nicosia, 1935.
Cyprus: Report on the Cyprus Police Force for the Year 1935, by W. C. C. King, Government Printing Office, Nicosia, 1936.

SELECT BIBLIOGRAPHY

Cyprus: Report on the Cyprus Police Force for the Year 1937, by W. S. Gulloch, Government Printing Office, Nicosia, 1938.
Hansard, House of Commons.
Minutes of the Legislative Council of Cyprus for 1929, Government Printing Office, Nicosia, 1930.
A Survey of Rural Life in Cyprus, by B. J. Surridge, Government Printing Office, Nicosia, 1930.

Anthologies

Asmussen, Jan, 'Disturbances in Cyprus in October, 1931', *Journal of Cyprus Studies*, 12, 2006, 5–55.
Papapolyviou, Petros (ed. & intro.), Υπόδουλοι Ελευθερωταί Αδελφών Αλυτρώτων: Πολεμικά Ημερολόγια, Επιστολές και Ανταποκρίσεις Κυπρίων Εθελοντών από την Ήπειρο και τη Μακεδονία του 1912–1913 (Enslaved Free Brother Soldiers: War Diaries, Letters and Responses of Cypriot Volunteers from Epirus and Macedonia 1912–1913), Nicosia, Cyprus Research Centre, 1999.
Solomonidou-Drousiotou, Antigoni, Η Ζωή μου σε Πρώτο Πρόσωπο (My Life in the First Person), Athens, Livani, 2004.

Unofficial Published Primary Sources

Newspapers

Australian: *Daily Mercury*; *Mercury*; *West Australian*.
Cyprus: Αλήθεια (Truth); Έθνος (Nation); Ελευθερία (Freedom); Κήρυξ (Crier); Κυπριακός Τύπος (Cypriot Press); Κύπρος (Cyprus); Νέος Κυπριακός Φύλαξ (New Cypriot Guardian); Νέων Έθνως (New Nation); Πατρίς (Country); Πάφος (Paphos); Πρωΐα (Morning); Πρωτεύουσα (Capital); Παρατηρητής (The Observer); Σάλπιγξ (Trumpet); Φωνή της Κύπρου (Voice of Cyprus); Χρόνος (Year); Ώρα (Time); *Cyprus Mail*.
Greece: Ανεξαρτιτός (Independent); Έστια (Focus); Λαϊκός Αγών (Popular Struggle); Πατρίς (Country); Πρωία (Morning); Καθημερινή (Everyday); Ελεύθερον Βήμα (Free Tribune).
UK: *Daily Express*; *The Times*; *Evening Telegraph*.
Straits Settlements: *The Straits Times*.

Books / Pamphlets

Azinas, Andreas, *50 Years of Silence: Cyprus' Struggle for Freedom: My EOKA Secret File*, Nicosia, Airwaves, 2002.
Balfour, Patrick (Lord Kinross), *The Orphaned Realm: Journeys in Cyprus*, London, Percival Marshall, 1951.
Cyprus: Touchstone for Democracy, Athens, Union of Journalists of the Athens Newspapers, November 1958.
Davidson, J. C. C., *Memoirs of a Conservative: J.C.C. Davidson's Memoirs and Papers, 1910–1937* (ed.) R. R. James, London, Weidenfeld & Nicolson, 1969.
Foley, Charles, *Island in Revolt*, London, Longmans, 1962.
———, *Legacy of Strife: Cyprus from Rebellion to Civil War*, Harmondsworth, Penguin, 1964.
Galatopoulos, Christodoulos Aristotle, *From the Cruiser to the Jail Birds' Nest* (ed. & intro., Petros Stylianou), Nicosia, Museum of Struggle, 1980.
Gialistras, Sergios A., *Hellas and Cyprus*, trans. G. A. Trypanis, Athens, 1955.
Grivas, George, *Guerrilla Warfare and EOKA's Struggle*, trans. A. A. Pallis, London, Longmans, 1964.

———, *The Memoirs of General Grivas*, ed. Charles Foley, London, Longmans, 1964.
Ioannou, Fifis, *Ετσι Ξεκίνησε το Κυπριακό: Στα Χνάρια μιας Δεκαετίας, 1940–1950* (Thus Began the Cyprus Conflict: In the Footsteps of a Decade, 1940–1950), Athens, Filistor, 2005.
Ipeirotou, Pyrros Giannopoulos, *Αι εκλογαί της 6 Δεκεμβρίου 1915: Πολιτικός λόγος* (The Elections of 6 December 1915: Political Reason), Athens, 1916.
———, *Οι Ιταλοί εν Ηπείρω* (The Italians in Ipeiros), Athens, 1917.
———, *Η Στάσις του Ιω. Μεταξά και ο Θρίαμβος της Επαναστάσεως του 1922* (The Stand of John Metaxas and the Triumph of the 1922 Revolution), Athens, 1923.
———, *Ο Κωνσταντινισμός και ο Μεταξάς* (Constantinism and Metaxas), Athens, 1926.
———, *Η Ρωσσία Καταρρευουσα: Η Ἑλλας Φραγμός εις την Σλαβικήν Επέκτασην* (The Russian Trajectory: Hellas as the Barrier to Slavic Expansion), Athens, 1949.
———, *Ενωτικοί Αγώνες της Κύπρου, 1878–1951* (Enosis Struggles of Cyprus, 1878–1951), Athens, 1951.
———, *Η Μάχη της Κύπρου, 1878–1956* (The Battle of Cyprus, 1878–1956), Athens, P. G. Ipeirotou, 1956.
Lanitis, Nicholas Kl., *Ο Ακρίτας του Ελληνικού Νότου* (Akritas of the Greek South), Athens, 1945.
———, *Η Δούλη Ελλάς του Νότου* (The Slaves of Hellas of the South), Athens, 1954.
Lekka, Tassos G., *Κύπρος: Η Κατεχόμενη Ἑλλας* (Cyprus: The Occupied Hellas), Athens, Dialismas, 1952.
Loizides, Savvas, *Άτυχη Κύπρος: Πως Έζησα τους Πόθους και τους Καημούς της 1910–1980* (Luckless Cyprus: How I Lived through Its Desires and Sorrows 1910–1980), Athens, Bergade, 1980.
———, *Cyprus Demands Self-Determination, National Committee for Self-Determination of Cyprus*, Athens, 1956.
———, *The Cyprus Question: Its Evolution – Present Aspects after the Plebiscite of January 1950*, Nicosia, 1950.
Mavrogordatos, George, *Stillborn Republic: Social Coalitions and Party Strategies in Greece, 1922–1936*, Berkeley: University of California Press, 1983.
Papaioannou, Ezekias, *Ενθημήσεις από την Ζωή Μου* (*Memories from My Life*), Nicosia, Pirsos, 1988.
Photias, N. G., *The Island of Cyprus*, Athens, Rotary Club of Athinai, 1956.
Rossides, Zenon G., *The Problem of Cyprus*, Athens, 1957.
Seraphim-Loizou, Elenitsa, *The Cyprus Liberation Struggle, 1955–1959: Through the Eyes of a Woman EOKA Area Commander*, trans. John Vickers, Nicosia, Epiphaniou, 2000 (first published in Greek, 1982).
Servas, Ploutis, *Κυπριακό: Ευθύνες* (Cyprus Problem: Responsibilities), Athens, Grammi, 1980.
Storrs, Sir Ronald, *Orientations*, London, Readers Union, 1939.
Swinton, Viscount (Philip Cunliffe-Lister), *I Remember*, London, Hutchinson, 1948.
Tsangarides, Theophanis, *Το Ημερολόγιου ενος Εξόριστου* (The Diary of an Exile), Athens, 1948.
Woodhouse, Christopher M., *Apple of Discord: A Survey of Recent Greek Politics in Their International Setting*, London, Hutchinson, 1948.

Articles / Book Chapters

Gwynn, Major-General Sir Charles W., *Imperial Policing*, London, 1936.

Loizides, Savvas, 'The Cyprus Question in the United Nations', *Revue Hellenique de Droit International*, 7, 1954, 214–19.

Nicholson, Reginald (Popham-Lobb), 'The Riots in Cyprus', *The Nineteenth Century*, 110, Dec. 1931, 685–93.

Secondary Sources

Monographs and Edited Volumes

Adams, T. W., *AKEL the Communist Party of Cyprus*, Stanford, Hoover Institute, 1971.

Alecou, Alexios, *Communism and Nationalism in Postwar Cyprus, 1945–1955*, New York, Palgrave Macmillan, 2016.

Anderson, Benedict, *Imagined Communities*, London, Verso, 1983.

Argyrou, Vassos, *Tradition and Modernity in the Mediterranean: The Wedding as Symbolic Struggle*, Cambridge, Cambridge University Press, 1996.

Asmussen, Jan, *Cyprus at War: Diplomacy and Conflict during the 1974 Crisis*, London, I.B. Tauris, 2008.

Badrawi, Malak, *Political Violence in Egypt, 1910–1924: Secret Societies, Plots and Assassinations*, Richmond, Curzon, 2000.

Ballantyne, Tony, *Webs of Empire: Locating New Zealand's Colonial Past*, Wellington, Bridget Williams, 2012.

Bryant, Rebecca, *Imagining the Modern: The Cultures of Nationalism in Cyprus*, London, I.B. Tauris, 2004.

Burton, Antoinette, *The Trouble with Empire: Challenges to Modern British Imperialism*, Oxford, Oxford University Press, 2015.

———, ed., *Archive Stories: Facts, Fictions, and the Writing of History*, Durham, Duke University Press, 2005.

Close, David, *The Origins of the Greek Civil War*, London, Longman, 1995.

Comaroff, Jean and John, *Ethnography and the Historical Imagination*, Boulder, Westview Press, 1992.

Coudounaris, Aristedis, *Βιογραφικόν Λεξικόν Κυπρίων, 1800–1920 (Biographical Lexicon of Cypriots, 1800–1920)*, Nicosia, Cyprus Research Centre, 2001.

Crawshaw, Nancy, *The Cyprus Revolt*, London, George Allen & Unwin, 1978.

Drousiotis, Makarios, *Cyprus 1974: Greek Coup and Turkish Invasion*, Mannheim und Mohnesee, Bibliopolis, 2006.

———, *The First Partition: Cyprus 1963–1964*, Nicosia, Alfadi, 2008.

French, David, *Fighting EOKA: The British Counter-Insurgency Campaign on Cyprus, 1955–1959*, Oxford, Oxford University Press, 2015.

Frendo, Henry, *Europe and Empire: Culture, Politics and Identity in Malta and the Mediterranean (1912–1946)*, Malta, Midsea, 2012.

Gallant, Thomas, *Modern Greece: From the War of Independence to the Present*, London, Bloomsbury, 2016.

Gellately, Robert, *Lenin, Stalin, and Hitler: The Age of Social Catastrophe*, New York, Knopf, 2007.

Georghallides, George S., *A Political and Administrative History of Cyprus*, Nicosia, Cyprus Research Centre, 1979.

———, *Cyprus and the Governorship of Sir Ronald Storrs: The Causes of the 1931 Crisis*, Nicosia, Cyprus Research Centre, 1985;
Heraclidou, Antigone, *Imperial Control in Cyprus: Education and Political Manipulation in the British Empire*, London, I.B. Tauris, 2017
Hill, George, *A History of Cyprus*, IV, (ed.) Sir Harry Luke, Cambridge, Cambridge University Press, 1952.
Holland, Robert, *Britain and the Revolt in Cyprus, 1954–1959*, Oxford, Oxford University Press, 1998.
Holland, Robert and Diana Markides, *The British and the Hellenes: Struggles for Mastery in the Eastern Mediterranean 1850–1960*, Oxford, Oxford University Press, 2006.
Ioannides, Christos P., *Cyprus under British Colonial Rule*, Lanham, Lexington, 2019.
James, Alan, *Keeping the Peace in the Cyprus Crisis of 1963–1964*, New York, Palgrave, 2001.
Katsiaounis, Rolandos, *Labour, Society and Politics in Cyprus during the Second Half of the Nineteenth Century*, Nicosia, Cyprus Research Centre, 1996.
———, *Η Διασκεπτική, 1946–1948: Με Ανασκόπηση της Περιόδου, 1878–1945* (The Consultative Assembly, 1946–48: With a Survey of the Period, 1878–1945), Nicosia, Cyprus Research Centre, 2000.
Katsourides, Yiannos, *The History of the Communist Party in Cyprus*, London, I.B. Tauris, 2014.
———, *The Greek Cypriot Nationalist Right in the Era of British Colonialism*, Springer, Cham, Switzerland, 2017.
Kelling, George Horton, *Countdown to Rebellion: British Policy in Cyprus, 1939–1955*, New York, Greenwood, 1990.
Kousouris, Dimitris, *Δίκες τών Δοσίλογων 1944–9* (Trials of Collaborationists 1944–1949), Athens, Polis, 2015.
Kyrris, Costas, *Peaceful Co-existence in Cyprus under British Rule (1878–1959) and after Independence*, Nicosia, PIO, 1977.
Leventis, Yiorghos, *Cyprus: The Struggle for Self-Determination in the 1940s*, Frankfurt, Peter Lang, 2002.
Llewellyn Smith, Michael, *Ionian Vision: Greece in Asia Minor, 1919–1922*, London, Hurst, 1973 (2nd ed. 1998).
Lockwood, David, *The Indian Bourgeoisie: A Political History of the Indian Capitalist Class in the Early Twentieth Century*, London, I.B. Tauris, 2012.
McKenzie, Kirsten, *Imperial Underworld: An Escaped Convict and the Transformation of the British Colonial Order*, Cambridge, Cambridge University Press, 2016.
Markides, Diana, *The Cyprus Tribute and Geopolitics in the Levant, 1875–1960*, Cham, Switzerland, Palgrave Macmillan, 2019.
Mazower, Mark, *Inside Hitler's Greece: The Experience of Occupation, 1941–44*, New Haven, Yale University Press, 1993.
Michaelidou, Agni, *Χώρα, η Παλιά Λευκωσία* (Country, Old Nicosia), Nicosia, 1974.
Morgan, Tabitha, *Sweet and Bitter Island: A History of the British in Cyprus*, London, I.B. Tauris, 2010.
Pafitou, Nadina, *Bank of Cyprus Chronicle, 1899–2009*, Nicosia, Bank of Cyprus, 2010.
Panteli, Stavros, *Place of Refuge: The History of the Jews in Cyprus*, London, Elliott & Thompson, 2003.
Papadakis, Yiannis, Nicos Peristianis and Gisela Welz (eds.), *Divided Cyprus: Modernity, History, and an Island in Conflict*, Bloomington and Indianapolis, Indiana University Press, 2006.

Papademetris, Panayiotis, *Ιστορική Εγκυκλοπαίδεια της Κύπρου, 1878–1978* (Historical Encyclopaedia of Cyprus, 1878–1978), Nicosia, 1979–80.

Papapolyviou, Petros, *Η Κύπρος και οι Βαλκανικοί πόλεμοι: Συμβολή στην ιστορία του κυπριακού εθελοντισμού* (Cyprus and the Balkan Wars: Contribution to the History of Cypriot Volunteerism), Nicosia, Cyprus Research Centre, 1997.

Peristiany, John G., *Honour and Shame: The Values of Mediterranean Society*, Chicago, University of Chicago Press, 1966.

Pikros, Ioannis, *Ο Βενιζέλος και το Κυπριακό* (Venizelos and the Cyprus Question), Athens, Philippotis, 1980.

Purcell, H. D., *Cyprus*, London, Ernest Benn, 1969.

Rappas, Alexis, *Cyprus in the 1930s: British Colonial Rule and the Roots of the Cyprus Conflict*, London, I.B. Tauris, 2014.

Richards, Eric, *The Last Scottish Food Riots*, Supplement No. 6, *Past & Present*, 1982.

Richter, Heinz, *Geschichte der Insel Zypern, 1878–1949* (History of the Island of Cyprus, 1878–1949), Vol. 1, Mannheim and Möhnesee, Bibliopolis, 2004.

Schmid, A. P. and A. J. Jongman et al., *Political Terrorism: A New Guide to Actors, Authors, Concepts, Data Bases, Theories, and Literature*, Amsterdam, North-Holland, Amsterdam, 1988.

Sigerson, S. M., *The Assassination of Michael Collins: What Happened at Béal na mBláth?* California, Createspace, 2013.

Stefanidis, Ioannides, D., *Isle of Discord: Nationalism, Imperialism and the Making of the Cyprus Problem*, New York, New York University Press, 1999.

Stoler, Ann Laura, *Along the Archival Grain: Epistemic Anxieties and Colonial Common Sense*, Princeton, Princeton University Press, 2010.

Stylianou, Petros, *Το Κίνημα του Οκτώβρη του 1931 στην Κύπρο* (The Movement of October of 1931 in Cyprus), Nicosia, P. Stylianou, 1984.

Vallianatos, Markos, *The Untold History of Greek Collaboration with Nazi Germany (1941–1944)*, Athens, Pelekys Books, 2014.

Varnava, Andrekos, *British Imperialism in Cyprus, 1878–1915: The Inconsequential Possession*, Manchester, Manchester University Press, 2009 (paperback, 2012).

———, *Serving the Empire in the Great War: The Cypriot Mule Corps, Imperial Identity and Silenced Memory*, Manchester, Manchester University Press, 2017 (paperback 2019).

———, *British Cyprus and the Long Great War, 1914–1925: Empire, Loyalties and Democratic Deficit*, London, Routledge, 2020.

Varnava, Andrekos and Hubert Faustmann (ed.), *Reunifying Cyprus: The Annan Plan and Beyond*, London, I.B. Tauris, 2009 (paperback 2011).

Varnava, Andrekos and Michalis N. Michael (eds.), *The Archbishops of Cyprus in the Modern Age: The Changing Role of the Archbishop-Ethnarch: Their Identities and Politics*, Newcastle upon Tyne, Cambridge Scholars Publishing, 2013.

Varnava, Andrekos, Nicholas Coureas and Marina Elia (eds.), *The Minorities of Cyprus: Development Patterns and the Identity of the Internal-Exclusion*, Newcastle upon Tyne, Cambridge Scholars Publishing, 2009.

Walsh, Michael and Andrekos Varnava (eds.), *The Great War and the British Empire: Culture and Society*, London, Routledge, 2017.

Wintle, Justin, *Perfect Hostage: A Life of Aung San Suu Kyi, Burma's Prisoner of Conscience*, New York, Skyhorse, 2007.

Xydis, Stephen, *Cyprus: Conflict and Conciliation, 1954–1958*, Columbus, Ohio State University, 1967.

———, *Cyprus: Reluctant Republic*, The Hague, Mouton, 1974.
Yiangou, Anastasia, *Cyprus in World War II: Politics and Conflict in the Eastern Mediterranean*, London, I.B. Tauris, 2010.
Zürcher, Erik, *The Young Turk Legacy and Nation Building: From the Ottoman Empire to Atatürk's Turkey*, London, I.B. Tauris, 2010.

Journal Articles

Anderson, David M., 'Mau Mau in the High Court and the "Lost" British Empire Archives: Colonial Conspiracy or Bureaucratic Bungle?' *The Journal of Imperial and Commonwealth History*, 39(5), 2011, 699–716.
Ball, Simon, 'The Assassination Culture of Imperial Britain, 1909–1979', *The Historical Journal*, 56(1), 2013, 231–56.
Banton, Mandy, '"Lost" and "Found": The Concealment and Release of the Foreign and Commonwealth Office "Migrated Archives"', *Comma*, 2012(1), 2012, 33–46.
———, 'Destroy? "Migrate"? Conceal? British Strategies for the Disposal of Sensitive Records of Colonial Administrations at Independence', *The Journal of Imperial and Commonwealth History*, 40(2), 2012, 321–35.
Bastian, Jeannette Allis, 'Reading Colonial Records through an Archival Lens: The Provenance of Place, Space and Creation', *Archival Science*, 6, 2006, 267–84.
Bowden, Tom, 'The Irish Underworld and the War of Independence 1919–21', *Journal of Contemporary History*, 8(2), 1973, 3–23.
Choumerianos, Manolis and Spyros Sakellaropoulos, 'The Communist Party of Cyprus, the Comintern and the Uprising of 1931: Thoughts on the "apologia" of Charalambos Vatyliotis (Vatis), *Twentieth Century Communism*, 16, 2019, 103–24.
Clarke, Peter and Andrekos Varnava, 'Accounting in Cyprus during British Rule, Post-World War I to Independence', *Accounting History*, 18(3), 2013, 293–315.
Georghallides, George S., 'Church and State in Cyprus, October 1931 to November 1932: A Systematic Humiliation of the Autocephalous Church of Cyprus?' *Annual of the Cyprus Research Centre*, 19, 1992, 361–448.
———, 'The Cyprus Revolt and the British Deportation Policy, October 1931-December 1932', *Kypriakai Spoudai*, 1993, 37–114.
Katsiaounis, Rolandos, 'Η Κυπριακή Παροικία του Λονδίνου και το Αρχιεπισκοπικό Ζήτημα της Κύπρου, 1928–1936' (The Cypriot Community of London and the Archiepiscopal Question of Cyprus, 1928–1936), *Annual of the Cyprus Research Centre*, 22, 1996, 521–56.
———, 'Τα Πρώτα Βήματα της Επιτροπής Κυπριακής Αυτονομίας' (The First Steps of the Committee for Cypriot Autonomy), *Annual of the Cyprus Research Centre*, 26, 2000, 263–87.
———, 'Cyprus 1931–1959: The Politics of the Anti-Colonial Movement', *Annual of the Cyprus Research Centre*, 2007, 441–69.
Katsourides, Yiannos, 'Anti-Colonial Struggle in Cyprus: Actors, Conceptualisations, Methods and Motives', *Journal of Mediterranean Studies*, 23(1), 2014, 31–46.
Kyrris, Costas, 'Symbiotic Elements in the History of the Two Communities of Cyprus', *Kypriakos Logos*, 8, 1976, 243–82.
Lal, V., 'Review: Subaltern Studies and its Critics: Debates Over Indian History', *History and Theory*, 40(1), 2001, 135–48.

Nasir, Kamaludeen Mohamed, 'Protected Sites: Reconceptualising Secret Societies in Colonial and Postcolonial Singapore', *Journal of Historical Sociology*, 29(2), 2016, 232–49.

Papadakis, Yiannis, 'The Politics of Memory and of Forgetting in Cyprus', *Journal of Mediterranean Studies*, 1993, 139–54.

———, 'Greek Cypriot Narratives of History and Collective Identity: Nationalism as a Contested Process', *American Ethnologist*, 25(3), 1998, 149–65.

Rappas, Alexis, 'The Uncharted World of Cypriot Colonial Servants and the Ideological Foundations of British Rule', *The Cyprus Review*, 23(2), 2011, 57–76.

———, 'The Cypriot Colonial Civil Servant: Practical Agency through Uncertain Identities', *The Cyprus Review*, 18(1), 2006, 121–36.

Sata, Shohei, '"Operation Legacy": Britain's Destruction and Concealment of Colonial Records Worldwide', *The Journal of Imperial and Commonwealth History*, 45(4), 2017, 1–23.

Smith, Evan and Andrekos Varnava, 'Creating a "Suspect Community": Monitoring and Controlling the Cypriot Community in London and their Immigration to the UK', *English Historical Review*, 132(557), 2017, 1149–81.

Stamelos, Harry, 'A Case Study of State and Law in the Interwar Period: The Three Historic Criminal Trials of Bishop of Paphos Leontios during the British Rule in Cyprus (1932, 1938, 1939)', *Athens Journal of Law*, 6(1), 2020, 75–102.

Stoler, Ann Laura, 'Colonial Archives and the Arts of Governance', *Archival Science*, 2, 2002, 87–109.

Varnava, Andrekos, 'The Impact of the Cypriot Contribution during the Great War on Colonial Society and Loyalties/Disloyalties to the British Empire', *First World War Studies*, 8(1), 2017, 17–36.

———, 'Greek Cypriot "Volunteers" in the Greek Army, 1897–1922: Querying Loyalties and Identity', forthcoming, *Journal of Modern Greek Studies*, 38(2), 2020.

———, 'The Origins and Prevalence of and Campaigns to Eradicate Venereal Diseases in British Colonial Cyprus, 1916–1939', *Social History of Medicine*, 33(1), 2020, 173–200.

Varnava, Andrekos and Peter Clarke, 'Accounting in Cyprus during Late Ottoman and Early British Rule, 1840–1918', *The Cyprus Review*, XXVI, 2, 2014, 33–55.

Varnava, Andrekos and Trevor Harris, ' "It is quite impossible to receive them": Saving the Musa Dagh Refugees and the Imperialism of European Humanitarianism", *Journal of Modern History*, 90(4), 2018, 834–62.

Book Chapters in Edited Volumes

Anagnostopoulou, Sia, 'Makarios III, 1950–77: Creating the Ethnarchic State', In Varnava and Michael, *The Archbishops of Cyprus in the Modern Age,,* 2013..

MacKenzie, John, 'The First World War and the Cultural, Political, and Environmental Transformation of the British Empire', In Walsh and Varnava, *The Great War and the British Empire*, 23–38.

Marovich-Old, Iliya, 'Nationalism as Resistance to Colonialism: A Comparative Look at Malta and Cyprus from 1919 to 1940', In *Cypriot Nationalisms in Context*, edited by Thekla Kyritsi and Nikos Christofis, 261–81.Cham, Palgrave Macmillan, 2018.

Michael, Michalis N., 'Panaretos, 1827–1840: His Struggle for Absolute Power during the Era of Ottoman Administrative Reforms'.In Varnava and Michael, *The Archbishops of Cyprus in the Modern Age* , 69–87.

Panayiotou, Andreas, 'Πως Εξαφανίζεται η Ιστορία: Το Πραξικόπημα του Κατεστημένου τον Ιούλιο του 1947 και οι Ρίζες του Ελληνοκυπριακού Βαθέως Κράτους της Δεξιάς' (How History Disappears: The Coup d'état of July 1947 and the Roots of the Deep Right-Wing Greek Cypriot State), forthcoming.

Papapolyviou, Petros, 'Ο Κυπριακός Εθελοντισμός στους Πολέμους της Ελλάδας, 1866–1945' ('Cypriot volunteerism in the wars of Greece, 1866–1945'). In *Κύπρος: Αγώνες Ελευθερίας στην Ελληνική Ιστορία* (Cyprus: Struggles for Freedom in Greek History), edited by Andreas I. Voskos, 204–29. Athens, 2010.Peristiany, J. G., 'Honour and Shame in a Cypriot Highland Village'. In *Honour and Shame: The Values of Mediterranean Society*, edited by J. G. Peristiany. University of Chicago Press, 1966 (repr. Midway, 1974).

Philippou, Stavroula and Andrekos Varnava, 'Constructions of Solution(s) to the Cyprus Problem: Exploring Formal Curricula in Greek-Cypriot State Schools'. In *Reunifying Cyprus: The Annan Plan and Beyond*, edited by Andrekos Varnava and Hubert Faustmann, 194–212. London, I.B. Tauris, 2009.

Pophaides, Irene, 'Kyrillos III, 1916–33: Between Sophronios III and Kyrillos II'. In Varnava and Michael, *The Archbishops of Cyprus in the Modern Age*, 177–209.

Rappas, Alexis, 'Leondios and the Archiepiscopal Question, 1933–47: The Demise of an Apolitical *Ethnarchy*?'. In Varnava and Michael, *The Archbishops of Cyprus in the Modern Age*, 211–39.

Robinson, R. E., 'Non-European Foundations of European Imperialism: Sketch for a Theory of Collaboration'. In *Studies in the Theory of Imperialism*, edited by Roger Owen and Robert B. Sutcliffe, 117–42. London: Longman, 1972.

Varnava, Andrekos, 'British and Greek Liberalism and Imperialism in the Long Nineteenth Century', In *Liberal Imperialism in Europe in the Long Nineteenth Century*, edited by Matthew Fitzpatrick, Studies in Intellectual and Cultural History, 219–40. London, Palgrave Macmillan, 2012.

Varnava, Andrekos, 'The Politics of Forgetting the Cypriot Mule Corps'. In *The Great War and the British Empire: Culture and Society*, edited by Michael J. K. Walsh and Andrekos Varnava, 291–303. London, Routledge, 2017.

Varnava, Andrekos, 'An Appraisal of the Works of Rolandos Katsiaounis: Society, Labour and Anti-Colonialism in Cyprus, 1850s-1950s'. In *Cypriot Nationalisms in Context: History, Identity, and Politics*, edited by Thekla Kyritsi and Nikos Christofi, 243–57. Cham, Palgrave Macmillan, 2018.

Varnava, Andrekos and Irene Pophaides, 'Kyrillos II, 1909–16: The First Greek Nationalist and *Enosist*', In Varnava and Michael, *The Archbishops of Cyprus in the Modern Age*, 148–76.

Varnava, Andrekos and Michalis N. Michael, 'Archbishop-*Ethnarchs* since 1767'. In Varnava and Michael, *The Archbishops of Cyprus in the Modern Age*, 1–16.

Varnava, Andrekos, 'Sophronios III, 1865–1900: The Last of the "Old" and the First of the "New" Archbishop-*Ethnarchs*?'. In Varnava and Michael, *The Archbishops of Cyprus in the Modern Age*, 106–47.

Varnava, Andrekos and Christalla Yakinthou, 'Cyprus: Political Modernity and Structures of Democracy in a Divided Island'. In *The Oxford Handbook of Local and Regional Democracy in Europe*, edited by John Loughlin, Frank Hendriks, and Anders Lidström, 455–77. Oxford University Press, Oxford, 2011.

Conference Proceedings

Chrysanthis, Kypros, 'Ιστορικά Δεδομένα σχετικά με το κίνημα του 1931' (Historical Facts on the movement of 1931), *Πρακτικά του Πρώτου Διεθνούς Κυπριολογικού Συνεδρίου, Λευκοσία 14–9 Απριλίου 1969* (First International Congress of Cypriot Studies, Nicosia 14–9 April 1969), 3(a), Nicosia, 1973, 451–56.

Georghallides, George S., 'British Policy on Cyprus During 1931', *Πρακτικά του Πρώτου Διεθνούς Κυπριολογικού Συνεδρίου, Λευκοσία 14–19 Απριλίου 1969* (First International Conference of Cypriot Studies, Nicosia 14–19 April 1969), 3(a), Nicosia, 1973, 96–104.

Dissertations

Papageorgiou, Thomas, *Η Κυπριακή Ενωτική Κίνηση στην Αθήνα, 1931–1940: Οι Βρετανικές Αντιδράσεις και η Στάση των Ελληνικών Κυβερνήσεων* (The Cyprus *Enosis* Movement in Athens, 1931–1940: The British Reaction and the Attitude of the Greek Governments), unpublished PhD dissertation, Aristotle University of Thessaloniki, 2014.

Voudouris, Athanasios G., *Το Εκκλησιαστικό Ζήτημα της Κύπρου κατά την Περίοδο 1933–1947* (The Church Question of Cyprus during the Period 1933–1947), unpublished PhD dissertation, Aristotle University of Thessaloniki, 2015.

Websites

Papademetris, Panayiotis: http://www.papademetris.net/

INDEX

Abbot, Charles Theodore 51, 53, 56, 58
Adamantos, Adam 97–98, 108
advisory council 1–5, 20, 40, 42–46, 50, 64–65, 68, 71, 75–77, 82–83, 93, 97–98, 105–6, 108
Agios Dometios 53
Agricultural Bank 28, 33
AKEL 11, 81, 85, 87–88, 93–101
Albania/Albania 89
Anastasiades, Costas 53, 55–56, 58, 81
Anastasiades, Petros 51
Androutsos, Christos 66
APOEL 24
Aradippiotis, George 40, 98, 108
Armenian Refugees 25
Ashiotis, Costas 48, 108
Ashmore, Jack 74–76, 78
Athens/Athenian 7, 19, 23, 29–30, 33, 40, 43, 59–61, 63, 66, 68–69, 72–74, 77, 80–81, 88–93, 96, 98–101, 103–4
Atlee, Clement 93

Balkan Wars 24, 32, 59, 82
Battershill, William 82, 90
Belcher, Charles Frederic 37
Blackall, Henry 18, 24, 39, 41, 51, 56, 61–63, 74, 78, 82, 103
Bulgaria/Bulgarian 89
Burma/Burmese 13

Cacoyannis, Panayiotis 28, 30, 40, 97–98
Cairo 95, 99
Ceylon 42
Christodoulou, Stavros 1, 6, 18, 21, 47, 53–60, 78–82, 104

Christofias, Demetris 88
Christou, Therapis 55, 58
Chrysafinis, George N. 98, 108
Chrysafinis, Nicholas G. 40, 51, 98, 108
Clerides, Glafkos 24, 107–8
Clerides, Ioannis 27–28, 30, 34, 39, 51, 65, 81, 83, 93, 97–99, 101, 107–9
Collins, Michael 13, 20
communism/communist 2–3, 11–13, 16–17, 19, 21, 37, 45, 52–56, 59–60, 76–83, 87–88, 90–95, 97–99, 102–3, 106–8, 110
Constantine, King of Greece 25, 2, 89
Constantinides, Paschalis 25–26
Constantinides, Phaedon 102
Coureas, Miltiades 27, 49, 57, 82, 96
Coureas, Nicholas (Historian) 58
Coureas, Nicholas S. 48–49, 52–53, 58, 67
CPC 11, 36–37, 80, 87, 95
Cuff, Cyril 57
Cunliffe-Lister, Philip 18, 40–41, 45, 61, 63, 76, 78, 80
Cypriot Brotherhood of St Barnabas (London) 88
Cypriot Civil War (1963–64) 87
Cypriot Mule Corps (Great War) 19, 86
Cypriot National Bureau (Athens) 59, 69
Cypriot Orthodox Church 12, 28–29, 45–46, 55, 61, 65–67, 80, 93, 97, 99, 102, 105, 108

Demetriades, Demetrios M. 48
Demetiou, Demetris N. 40, 108
Democratic Union 101
Denktaş, Rauf Raif 51

Dervis, Themistocles N. 12, 40, 47, 49, 63, 66, 81–82, 90–91, 95–97, 99, 101, 107–8
Dikomo 53, 59, 80

Egypt/Egyptian 7–8, 69
EOKA 3, 5, 10, 12–13, 18, 20–21, 23–24, 44, 85–102, 104, 106–7
Epirus 59
Evangelides, Socrates E. 98
executive council 3, 30, 32–35, 40, 42, 59, 72, 92, 98, 101, 104

Far Left 8, 11, 13–14, 78, 85, 87–88, 93–101, 107
Far Right/Extremists 3, 6, 8, 10–15, 18–21, 30, 33–35, 36–42, 53, 55, 57, 59–60, 63, 65, 67–68, 72, 78, 80–83, 86–94, 96–99, 102–3, 106–10
fascism, xii 80, 92
Famagusta 36, 38, 42, 51, 54, 75, 97, 102, 109
Fasouliotis, Panos 48–49
FBIS 95
Fieros, Constantine 98, 108
FIFA 24
Foley, Charles 23, 90
Fuad Bey 51

Galatopoulos, Christodoulos Aristotle 39, 72
Germany/German 68, 89, 91
Gibraltar 7–8
Göttingen 31
Great Depression 33, 36
Great War/First World War 11, 19–20, 86
Greece/Greek 9–14, 21, 24, 27, 37, 64, 66, 69–70, 74, 86, 89–101, 105
Greek Civil War 12, 94, 109
Greek Junta (1967–74) 24, 88
Greek War of Independence 31
Grivas, George 92, 100–101
Gunnis, Rupert 51

Hadji Pavlou, George 27–32
Hadji Procopi, Hadji Eftychios 29–30
Hart-Davis, Charles 38, 51, 82

Hamilton, Lord George 14
Henniker-Heaton, Herbert 51, 57, 62, 82
Heidelberg 31
Hitler, Adolf 68, 77
Hong Kong 41, 45

Iakovides, Nicholas 96
Ioannides, Fedon 28
Ioannides, Polycarpos Stylianou 6, 35, 43, 52, 59, 64, 76, 80–82, 91, 94, 101, 104
Ioannides, Pygmalion 52, 64, 78, 80–81
Ioannou, Fifis 97, 108
Ipeirotou, Pyrrou Giannopoulou 89, 91
Italy/Italian 89, 109

Jamaica 45
Jews/Jewish 68

Kakoullis, Kyriakos 48
Karamanlis, Constantine 101
Karavas 59
Katalanos, Nicholas 25
KEK (Cypriot Nationalist Party) 12, 85, 90–91, 95, 97–99
Kennedy, John F. 20
Kennedy, Robert F. 20
King Jr., Martin Luther 20
King, William C. C. 57, 67–68, 70, 74, 78–79, 81
Kolokasides, Theodoros 36, 40, 61, 63, 73, 80, 88, 99, 104
Kykkotis, Archimandrite Ierotheos 66, 73
Kyprianou, Spyros 88
Kyrenia 1, 7, 19, 21, 26, 30–31, 36, 43, 52–53, 59–60, 64–65, 77, 94, 98, 101, 104, 109
Kyriakides, Stella 24, 110
Kyrillos II, Archbishop of Cyprus 32, 47
Kyrillos III, Archbishop of Cyprus 25, 37, 39–40, 47, 65, 105
Kyrou, Achilles 70, 91
Kyrou, Alexis 35, 70, 80, 91

Lanitis, Nicholas C. 98
Lanitis, Nicholas P. 40
Larnaca 1, 44, 51, 53, 63, 74–75, 77, 97–98, 109

INDEX

Ledra St. 67
legislative council 2–3, 27–35, 39–42, 44, 56, 104, 108
Leontios, Archbishop; Bishop of Paphos; *Locum Tenens* 12, 21, 39, 49, 62, 65, 93–99, 106
Limassol 31, 33, 40, 42, 48, 51–52, 62–63, 95, 109
Loizides, Savvas 7, 18, 30, 32–40, 42, 59, 61, 63–64, 69, 72–73, 76, 80, 83, 88, 91–93, 96, 99–101, 104
Loizides, Socrates 100
Loizou, Savvas 54–55
Louisides, Michalakis J. 42, 75
Lysandrides, Sophocles 49

Makarios II, Archbishop of Cyprus; Bishop of Kyrenia 7, 19, 26, 29–31, 35–37, 39–40, 43, 59, 63–66, 69, 73, 80–81, 88–89, 91–99, 102, 104–5, 107
Makarios III, Archbishop of Cyprus; Bishop of Kitium 24, 47, 88, 99–101, 107
Malta/Maltese 4, 7–9, 13, 27, 40, 107–9
Markides, Alecos 110
Markides, George 27–28, 52, 64, 76, 81–82
Mathaiou, Pantelis 55, 80
Mavros, Sotiris Antoniou 54–58
Maximos, Demetrios 68
Mehmet Bey, Raif 51, 56
Melissas, Menelaos 51
Metaxas, Ioannis 69, 89, 93
Mintoff, Dom 108
Montagu, James Drogo 82
Morphou 29, 97

National Liberation Coalition (NLC) 97–98
National Radical Union (Greece) 101
National Radical Union Cyprus (EREK) 6, 10, 12, 31, 35–37, 43, 59, 64, 73, 79, 76, 81, 90, 94, 100–101, 104
Nazi/Nazism 31, 68, 77, 91–93, 100
Nicodemos, Bishop of Kitium 36–37, 61, 65–66, 73, 105

Nicolaides, Neophytos 29–30, 40, 42
Nicolaides, Nicholas 76
Nicosia 1–2, 18, 23–25, 34, 37–38, 42, 47–59, 62, 65, 68, 77, 79, 81, 90, 94, 96–99, 109
Nigeria 79, 82
Nikopoulos, Polycarpos 97, 108

Olivier, George Borg 108
Operation Legacy 2, 16
Organisation 'X' 12, 92–95, 98–99

Palestine 7–8
Palmer, Herbert Richmond 12, 51–53, 61–69, 72, 74–78, 80–83, 90, 97, 103
Papadopoulos, Stelios G. 49, 57
Papadopoulos, Tassos 88
Papaioannou, Ezekias 95
Papa Nicolaou, Evagoras 35, 43, 52, 59, 64, 81–82, 94, 96–97, 104
Paphos 28, 39, 42, 52, 65, 76, 109
Parkinson, Cosmo 78, 85, 97
Paschalis, Neoptolemos 26–40, 51, 53, 56, 58, 62–63, 65, 69, 71, 83, 98, 103, 108
Pavlides, George 42
Pavides, Kyrillos K. 40
Pavlides, Maria 103
Pavlides, Paul George 98, 108
Pavlides, Stelios 28–36, 40, 42, 51, 68–69, 71, 98, 103, 108
Pavlou, Savvas 55
People's Party (Greece) 68
Petrou, Theodosios 88
Philippou, Loizos 28, 35, 40, 98
Photios II, Ecumenical Patriarch 66
Pigasiou, Ioannis 27, 29, 35, 52, 54–56, 58–60, 64, 76, 78–82, 103–4
Pitrakkou, Antonis, xiii 85
Poullos, Nikos 55, 58

Ramsay, Patrick 66

Sampson, Nicos 6, 24
San, Aung 13
Santamas, Lysos 97–98, 108
Second World War 4, 12, 57, 99, 102, 106–7, 109

Sertsios, Basil 51
Servas, Ploutis 95, 97–98, 108
Severis, Christodoulos 17
Severis, Costas 98, 108
Severis, Demosthenis 24, 28, 40, 61, 98, 108
Severis, Maria 24, 61
Severis, Zenon 17, 98, 108
Seychelles 101
Singapore 14
Skouriotissa 54
socialism/socialist 12, 37, 39, 48, 89
Sozos, Christodoulos 32
Spyridakis, Ioannis 96
Stanley, Oliver 93
Stavrinakis, Stavros G. 28, 30, 56, 58, 108
Stavrinides, Demosthenis 45, 48, 66, 73
Stavrinides, Stavros E. 51, 108
Stevenson, Malcolm 27, 32
Storrs, Ronald 5, 18, 32, 34, 37–40, 59, 89
Strong, Herbert 51, 56, 58
Stubbs, Reginald 40–42, 45–46, 51
Surridge, Brewser Joseph 63, 77, 104

Theodotou, Eugenia 75
Theodotou, Theophanis 5, 7, 17, 26, 28, 30, 32, 34, 37, 41, 61, 63, 72–75
Tingiris, Sophocles 51
TMT 13, 87
Tornaritis, Criton G. 51, 98, 108
Triantafyllides, Antis A. 24, 98

Triantafyllides, Christos M. 24
Triantafyllides, Loulla 61, 68
Triantafyllides, Michalakis A. 1–2, 19, 21, 23–24, 57–58, 103, 104, 108
Triantafyllides, Solon A. 24
Tsangarides, Theophanis 18, 35–36, 40, 61, 63, 73, 80, 88, 99, 104
Tseriotis, Panayiotis 98, 108
Turkey/Turkish/Ottoman Empire 4, 8, 12, 14, 23, 88–89

USSR/Soviet Russia/Soviet Union 11, 37, 89

Valdaserides, Michael 40, 75
Vassiliades, George 40, 83, 97, 108
Vassiliou, George 23, 88, 110
Venizelos, Eleftherios/Venizelist/anti-Venizelist 1, 2, 5, 13, 25, 27, 35, 39, 48, 88–89, 105

Waterlow, Sydney 68, 70, 80
Winster, Lord (Reginald Fletcher) 93, 95, 98
Woolley, Charles Campbell 92–93
Wyllie, Curzon 14

X, Malcolm 20

Zemenides, Angelos 21, 88–89, 94, 106
Zemenides, Euripides 94, 96, 99
Zurich-London Accords (1959) 101

www.ingramcontent.com/pod-product-compliance
Lightning Source LLC
Chambersburg PA
CBHW032052150426
43194CB00006B/503